HARDPRESS.NET

ISBN: 9781290528641

Published by:
HardPress Publishing
8345 NW 66TH ST #2561
MIAMI FL 33166-2626

Email: info@hardpress.net
Web: http://www.hardpress.net

The Medical Epitome Series.

MICROSCOPY AND BACTERIOLOGY.

A MANUAL FOR STUDENTS AND PRACTITIONERS.

BY

P. E. ARCHINARD, A. M., M. D.,

Demonstrator of Microscopy and Bacteriology, Tulane University of Louisiana, Medical Department.

SERIES EDITED BY

V. C. PEDERSEN, A. M., M. D.,

Instructor in Surgery and Assistant Anæsthetist at the New York Polyclinic Medical School and Hospital; Deputy Genito-Urinary Surgeon to the Out-Patient Department of the New York Hospital; Physician-in-Charge, St. Chrysostom's Dispensary; Anæsthetist to the Roosevelt Hospital (First Surgical Division).

ILLUSTRATED WITH SEVENTY-FOUR ENGRAVINGS.

LEA BROTHERS & CO.,

PHILADELPHIA AND NEW YORK.

ELECTROTYPED BY
WESTCOTT & THOMSON, PHILADA.

PRESS OF
WM. J. DORNAN, PHILADA.

AUTHOR'S PREFACE.

THE scope of an Epitome of Bacteriology and Microscopy obviously affords little or no opportunity for original work, nor indeed would it be desirable to do more than represent the actual status of these cognate sciences. Standard text-books have accordingly been consulted freely. The merit of an Epitome consists in affording a concise and clear presentation of essentials, command of which enables the student to build a sound superstructure of knowledge. The practitioner may also use such a volume to post himself on the main facts of Bacteriology and Microscopy, and the technique. The list of questions appended to each chapter will be useful to students in quizzing and reviewing.

P. E. A.

NEW ORLEANS, 1903.

EDITOR'S PREFACE.

In arranging for the editorship of *The Medical Epitome Series* the publishers established a few simple conditions, namely, that the Series as a whole should embrace the entire realm of medicine; that the individual volumes should authoritatively cover their respective subjects in all essentials; and that the maximum amount of information, in letter-press and engravings, should be given for a minimum price. It was the belief of publishers and editor alike that brief works of high character would render valuable service not only to students, but also to practitioners who might wish to refresh or supplement their knowledge to date.

To the authors the editor extends his heartiest thanks for their excellent work. They have fully justified his choice in inviting them to undertake a kind of literary task which is always difficult—namely, the combination of brevity, clearness, and comprehensiveness. The authors have shown a consistent interest in the work and an earnest endeavor to coöperate with the editor throughout the undertaking. Co-operation of this kind ought to result in useful books, in brief manuals as contradistinguished from mere compends. The editor desires at this opportunity to express his appreciation of their helpfulness in the matter of producing the proper character of work.

In order to render the volumes suitable for quizzing, and yet preserve the continuity of the text unbroken by the interpolation of questions throughout the subject-matter, which has heretofore been the design in books of this type, all questions have been placed at the end of each chapter. This new arrangement, it is hoped, will be convenient alike to students and practitioners.

VICTOR C. PEDERSEN.

NEW YORK, 1903.

CONTENTS.

INTRODUCTION.

CHAPTER I.

CHAPTER VII.

CHAPTER VIII.

CHAPTER IX.

CHAPTER X.

CHAPTER XIX.

CHAPTER XX.

CHAPTER XXI.

CHAPTER XXII.

CHAPTER XXIII.

CHAPTER XXIV.

MICROSCOPY AND BACTERIOLOGY.

INTRODUCTION.

THE REFRACTION OF LIGHT AND THE MICROSCOPE.

THE REFRACTION OF LIGHT.

Definition.—Refraction is the property possessed by transparent media of altering the rays of light which pass through them. It is to this property possessed by lenses, the transparent media of microscopes, that these instruments owe their magnifying power.

The Two Fundamental Laws of Refraction.

I. When a ray of light passes from a denser to a rarer medium, it is refracted away from a line drawn perpendicularly to the plane which divides the media; and *vice versa*, when the light passes from a rarer to a denser medium, it is refracted toward that perpendicular.

II. The sines of the angles of incidence and refraction—that is, of the angles which the ray makes with the perpendicular before and after its refraction—bear to one another a constant ratio for each substance, which is known as its index of refraction.

The Principles of Refraction by Lenses.

Microscope lenses are **chiefly convex**; those of other forms are used to make certain modifications in the rays passing through the convex lens, and so render their performance more exact.

Focus of a Lens.—For a lens to give a perfect image of an object, all the rays of light coming from that object and passing through the lens must meet at the same point on the other side of the lens. This point is known as the focal point or focus of the lens.

The Spherical Aberration of Lenses.

Definition.—It is difficult, however, so to construct a convex lens that all the rays of light that pass through it shall come to the same focus. As a rule, the rays which traverse its peripheral or marginal portion come to a shorter focus than those which pass through its more central portion.

Correction.—Distortion of the image is thus caused, and is known as spherical aberration. Theoretically, spherical aberration might be corrected by making the curvature of the periphery of the lens less than that of its more central portion; but the difficulties in the mechanical construction of such a lens would be very great, and opticians have found it more practical to correct this defect by coupling with a convex lens a concave one of less curvature, but which is subject to exactly the opposite error of refraction.

Doublets.—These combinations of convex and concave lenses, or doublets, act as a single convex lens.

Triplets.—Sometimes two convex and one concave lens are used in combination, and are called triplets.

The Chromatic Aberration of Lenses.

Definition.—When light traverses a convex lens, the different colors which compose it do not all come to the same focus —that is, the colors are of unequal refrangibility; and the image then is seen chiefly in that color which chances to be in focus. This color-distortion is especially noticeable with the marginal rays, and is known as chromatic aberration.

Correction.—Though exclusion of the marginal rays can, as with spherical aberration, partly correct this defect, yet this is not sufficient, and chromatic aberration is remedied best by constructing the convex lenses of the combination mentioned above of crown glass, and the concave lenses of flint glass, as those two kinds of glass have opposite properties with regard to refrangibility.

THE MICROSCOPE.

Microscopes are of **two kinds**: simple and compound:

The Simple Microscope.

The ordinary hand magnifying-glass and the dissecting microscope are **examples** of simple microscopes.

Their **magnifying power** depends upon one lens or several lenses acting as one double convex lens. To obtain a clear, enlarged image of the object, the latter must be in its **principal focus**, and the shorter the focus of the lens the greater its magnifying power. The **focal length**, or **focus**, of the lens depends on the degree of curvature of the lens.

In **expressing the magnifying power of lenses**, the size of an object as seen by the unaided eye at ten inches distance is taken as unity. A lens having a magnifying power of ten diameters, or linears, is one which enlarges the object ten times in each linear direction.

The Compound Microscope.

The compound, or ordinary, microscope consists of the **stand** and **lenses**.

The **stand** comprises the following parts:

1. **Base** or **foot**;
2. **Pillars**, or **upright**, which may be jointed or not;
3. Arm connecting the pillars with the—
4. **Body**, containing the—
5. **Draw-tube**; moved up and down rapidly or slowly by means of the—
6. **Coarse adjustment**—used to bring the object into view;
7. **Fine adjustment**—used only when the object is already in view, to bring out more clearly its details.

8. **Stage**—the flat part on which is laid the object to be examined, and which is perforated by a central hole to allow illumination of the object from below. The stage may be **circular** or **square, stationary** or **movable**, and **mechanical.**

Underneath the Stage are Found the Parts:

9. **Flat mirror** for low-power, and

10. **Concave mirror** for high-power objectives.

The mirror is so arranged as to allow motion in all directions. For ordinary histological purposes it is usually fixed perpendicularly to the stage, and gives *direct light;* occasionally it is placed in an oblique direction, giving *oblique light.*

11. **Diaphragm.**—Immediately below the stage and about two inches above the mirror, though freely movable up and down, is found the diaphragm or **stop**: used to prevent the peripheral or diffuse rays of light from the mirror from reaching the object, and to allow only the more central and direct rays to illuminate the same. The holes in the diaphragm are of different sizes, the smaller ones being used with the higher power and the larger ones with the lower power class of work.

12. **Condenser.**—For very high powers, especially such as are used in bacteriology, besides the foregoing parts, there are on the substage the condenser, which is a lens, or system of lenses, used to concentrate still further the light from the mirror on the object. The condenser most commonly in use is known by the name of its introducer as the Abbe. The condenser should be exactly central, and, as a rule, it should be brought almost into contact with the object on the stage.

13. **Iris Diaphragm.**—Immediately below the condenser, instead of the ordinary diaphragm, what is known as an iris diaphragm is used (so called from its peculiar variability, like the iris of the eye).

14. **Nose-piece or Revolver.**—At the bottom of the tube a mechanical piece, which enables one to attach two or three objectives to the microscope at the same time, is known as the nose-piece or revolver.

15. **Lenses.**—These are so important that a detailed description of them is necessary.

The Lenses and Lens-systems of the Microscope.

Lenses.—The lenses of an ordinary microscope are of **two kinds**: those attached to the end of the tube nearer the object, and known by the name of the **objective lens**, or **objective system of lenses**, and those fitting the end of the tube into which the observer looks, known as the **eye-piece** or **ocular lens.**

The Objective Lens or System of Lenses.

The **objective** is the principal lens or system of lenses of the microscope. It is that which gives the greatest part of the magnifying power to the instrument. As ordinarily arranged, it is **composed** of a number of lenses connected together in various ways, and known as combinations or systems. The combination nearest the object is called the **front combination,** or **front lens,** and that nearest the ocular the **back combination,** or **back lens.** There may be one or more **intermediate systems** between these. Each combination, or system, consists of a concave lens of flint glass and a convex lens of crown glass; the whole combination acts as a double convex lens. The purposes of having lenses of various shapes and materials is to correct what is known as chromatic (colored) and spherical aberration or distortion (see Fig. 1).

Designation of the Objective.—Objectives are designated, as a rule, by their equivalent focal lengths. This length is usually given in inches or fractions thereof—for instance, 1 inch, $\frac{1}{3}$ inch, $\frac{1}{7}$ inch. In continental Europe the numerator of the fraction is often omitted, the $\frac{1}{3}$ objective being called 3, and the $\frac{1}{7}$ inch being called 7. These numbers indicate that the objective produces a real image of the same size as is produced by a simple convex lens whose principal focal distance would be that indicated by the number. And as "the relative size of object and image vary directly as their distance

Fig. 1.

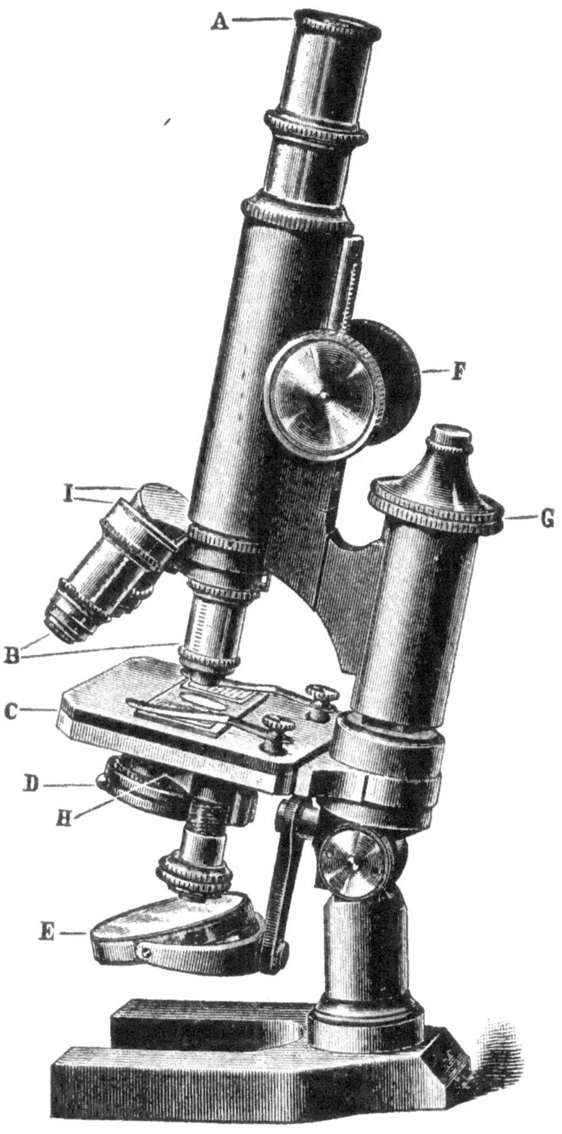

Microscope: A, ocular or eye-piece; B, objective system; C, stage; D, iris diaphragm (its opening may be diminished or increased by means of a small lever); E, mirror or reflector; F, coarse adjustment; G, fine adjustment; H, substage condenser (Abbe's); I, nose-piece.

from the centre of the lens," the less the equivalent focal distance of the objective, the greater is its magnifying power.

An objective of $\frac{1}{3}$ inch, or No. 3, therefore, magnifies less than one of $\frac{1}{7}$ inch, or No. 7.

The **working distance of the microscope**—that is, the distance between the objective and the object—is always less than the equivalent focal distance of the objective.

The Types of Objective Lens.

1. **Dry and Immersion Objectives.**

In the **dry objectives,** nothing intervenes between the objective and the object to be examined except air: all low-power objectives are dry.

In the **immersion objectives,** some liquid, such as water, glycerin, or oil (**homogeneous immersion objectives**), must be placed upon the cover-glass over the object and make contact between the cover-glass and the objective. Such lenses are known, respectively, as **water-, glycerin-,** and **oil-immersion lenses.** In homogeneous immersion objectives the oil has the same refracting index as the front lens of the objective.

2. **Non-achromatic objectives** are objectives in which the color-distortion is not corrected, and the image produced is bordered by a colored fringe; they also show spherical distortion.

3. **Achromatic objectives** are those in which the color-aberration is corrected.

4. **Aplanatic objectives** are those in which the spherical aberration is corrected. All better classes of objectives are both achromatic and aplanatic.

5. **Apochromatic objectives** are objectives in which rays of three spectral colors combine at one focus instead of rays of two colors, as in the ordinary achromatic. They are highly achromatic objectives.

6. **Adjustable objectives** are objectives in which the distance between the front and back combinations may be regulated by means of a milled-head screw. This is useful in dry or water-immersion objectives to correct the dispersion of light caused by different thicknesses of the cover-glasses.

The **angular aperture of an objective** is the angle formed between the most diverging rays issuing from the axial point of an object that may enter and take part in the formation of an image. By **axial point** is meant a point situated in the extended optical axis of the microscope.

The **optical axis** of the microscope is a line drawn from the eye through the middle of the tube to the centre of the objective.

Relation of Size and Working Distance of the Lens.—The larger the lens and the less its working distance, the greater the angle of aperture. For dry objectives the greater the angular aperture, the better the definition of the objective.

Numerical aperture is the capacity of an optical instrument for receiving rays from the object and transmitting them to the image, and the numerical aperture of a microscopic objective is, therefore, determined by the ratio between its focal length and the diameter of the emergent pencil at the point of its emergence—that is, the utilized diameter of a single-lens objective or of the back lens of a compound objective. It is the ratio of the diameter of the emergent pencil to the focal length of the lens, or, in other words, it is the index of refraction of the medium in front of the objective multiplied by the sine of half the aperture.

The Ocular Lens or Eye-piece.

The eye-piece, or ocular, is the lens, or combination of lenses, placed in the tube at the point of observation. It acts as a simple microscope and serves to magnify the image of the object. The ocular consists of two lenses, one situated nearer the eye, known as the eye-lens, and the other known as the field-lens. The ocular is said to be positive when the image is formed beyond it; and negative when it is formed within it, between the field-lens and eye-lens. In the positive ocular the two lenses act together as a simple microscope and magnify the image. In the negative ocular the field-lens acts with the objective in making clearer the image, and with the eye-lens in helping to correct some of the aberrations. The eye-lens also magnifies the image.

The Types of Ocular Lens.

1. **Compensating oculars,** which correct the chromatic aberration of the ray outside of the axis.

2. **Projecting oculars,** used with the projecting microscope or for microphotography.

3. **Spectroscopic oculars.**

These three types, among many, are the most important and most frequently employed.

The **designation of oculars** is by their **magnifying power** and **equivalent focal distance,** and also by numbers, the smaller number designating the lower power, and *vice versa.*

The **field of the microscope** is the lighted portion which is seen when one looks through the microscope with the instrument in focus.

The **eye-point** is the distance from the instrument at which the eye may look through with the least strain.

The Care of the Microscope.

Keep the instrument cleaned, and see that all mechanical parts move smoothly and evenly. Keep the mirror, condenser, and diaphragm central—that is, in the optical axis. Bring the object into view with the coarse adjustment, and define the details in it by means of the fine adjustment. See that no dirt or dust of any kind covers the lenses. Should the field be blurred or dim, after proper focusing and lighting, the fault is either with the lenses or the cover-glass is soiled.

Tests for the Sources of Dimness in the Object.—By revolving the ocular with the eye in position, the dimness, when due to the ocular, will also move. By moving gently the object with the hands, the dimness will move if due to dirt on the cover-glass. Should the blurring be stationary in both the above tests, it is due to soiling of the objective.

To **cleanse the lenses of the ocular,** blow on both surfaces of each lens and wipe dry with a fine silk handkerchief, old soft linen rag, or, better, rice-paper. To **cleanse the objective,** wipe, put the lens into the instrument and test it as described in the preceding paragraph, and if this is not sufficient, pass a little water or absolute alcohol over the surface and wipe dry. If the soiling is due to balsam or other resinous substance, clean gently with benzole or xylol. The back surface of the objective need never get dirty; but when it does, inserting a soft rag into the objective and gently turning it around is sufficient to cleanse it. *Never screw apart the different lenses of the objective, as it takes an expert optician to put them into proper position.* Always see that the cover-glass is clean and dry on its upper surface. Never bring the front lens of the objective into direct contact with the object or cover-glass.

For **bacteriological work,** it is indispensable to have a microscope supplied with an Abbe condenser and an oil-immersion objective of $\frac{1}{12}$ inch focus.

Different objectives according to their construction require different **tube-lengths of the microscope** to magnify at their fullest power and give their best definition. Manufacturers generally supply full information as to the proper tube-length for each instrument.

QUESTIONS.

What is refraction?
Give the two laws of refraction.
What is the type of the microscope lenses?
What is the focus of a lens?
What is meant by spherical aberration? How is this corrected?
What are doublets and triplets?
What is meant by refrangibility? How is this corrected in microscope lenses?
How many kinds of microscope are there?
What is a simple microscope?
How is the magnifying power of lenses expressed?
What is meant by a compound microscope?
Give the different parts of a compound microscope?
What is meant by direct light?
What purpose does a diaphragm serve?
What is a condenser?
What is meant by an iris diaphragm?
What is a nose-piece?
How are the lenses of an ordinary microscope called?
What is an objective?
How many lenses or combinations of lenses does an ordinary objective contain?
How is the magnifying power of objectives designated?

What is meant by the focal distance of an objective? The working distance?

What is the difference between the dry and immersion objectives?

What is a homogeneous immersion objective?

What is meant by a non-achromatic objective?

What is meant by an achromatic objective? An aplanatic objective?

What is an apochromatic objective?

What is meant by an adjustable objective?

What is the angular aperture of an objective?

What is meant by the actual point of an objective?

What is the optical axis of a microscope?

What relation does the size of the lenses have to its angular aperture?

What is the numerical aperture of an objective? What is the ocular of a microscope?

Of how many lenses does it consist?

What is the difference between the positive and the negative ocular.

What is a compensating ocular? A projecting?

How are oculars designated?

What is the field of a microscope?

What is the eye-point?

What care should be given to a microscope?

Describe the tests for determining the cause of an obscure image.

Describe the methods of cleansing the lenses of the microscope.

CHAPTER I.

THE FUNDAMENTAL PRINCIPLES.

THE HISTORY OF BACTERIOLOGY.

WHEN in the latter part of the seventeenth century **Anthony von Leuwenhoek**, by means of his magnifying-glasses, first discovered organisms in decaying vegetable infusions, he may be said to have laid the very first stone in the foundation of what later on was to be the Science of Bacteriology.

It was very long after this, however, before sufficient facts were collected to place this science upon a firm basis, and it remained for a genius like the immortal **Pasteur** and the eminent talents of the equally great **Koch** to build up the superstructure of bacteriology so as to have it accepted by all as the true basis of scientific medicine.

When first observed, these *microörganisms were supposed*

to be animalcules, and were accepted as such until the middle of the nineteenth century, when **F. Cohn** classed them *as belonging to the vegetable kingdom*, and listed them among the fungi, making of them the third variety of fungi, the **schizomycetes** or **cleft fungi**; the other two being the **saccharomycetes** or **sprouting fungi** (the yeast plant), and the **hyphomycetes** or **mucorini** (the moulds).

THE CLASSIFICATION OF COHN FOR BACTERIA.

This, as just given, is accepted to-day by all authorities, though it is open to criticism. Although it is true that the great majority of these organisms like the fungi possess no chlorophyl, and are unable, like other vegetables, to obtain their nourishment from the carbon dioxide and nitrogen of the atmosphere, but, on the contrary, like animals, require higher carbohydrate and nitrogenous substances, which they decompose into their primitive elements for their subsistence. A few of them, however, possess some plant coloring-matter, and some seem able to thrive in a simple saline solution from which absolutely no nitrogen is to be obtained.

THE DEFINITION OF "BACTERIA."

The proper name therefore for these organisms, and the one generally adopted, is **bacteria**, which is the plural of the Latin substantive **bacterium**. They may be **defined** as follows: *Unicellular vegetables of low organization, devoid of chlorophyl (plant coloring-matter), and multiplying by fission.*

The **bacteria cells** consist of a **cell-membrane** and **protoplasm**, which latter is sometimes clear and sometimes granular, but with no nuclei. The **cell-membrane** is a firm, tough envelope, very much like cellulose, which occasionally in some bacteria becomes viscid and gelatinous in its outer layers, forming a sort of bright halo around the bacteria, called a capsule. This gelatinous matter occasionally serves to bind two or more bacteria together, and gives to them quite a characteristic grouping which helps to distinguish them from others. In some instances the membranous envelope interferes considerably with the staining of the protoplasm of the bacteria cells, so that special methods of staining have to be adopted for these. Again, those bacteria which are generally found surrounded by a **capsule**, when grown in artificial media seem to lose the power of developing capsules.

THE MORPHOLOGICAL CLASSIFICATION OF BACTERIA.

Bacteria are divided into three varieties: (1) the rounded form or coccus (plural cocci); (2) the rod-shaped form or bacillus (plural bacilli); and (3) the curved or spiral form, spirillum (plural spirilla).

I. The Coccus.

Varieties.—The cocci, which are not always round, but very often oval in form, are further distinguished according as they appear: singly and of large size, as **megacocci**; of small size, as **micrococci**; double—that is, two of the cells adhering together, as **diplococci**; in chains—that is, a number of cells adhering together in single file—as **streptococci**; in groups very like a bunch of grapes, as **staphylococci**; in groups of four, as **tetrads or merismopedia**; in groups of eight arranged in cubes, as **sarcinæ**; in irregular masses united by an intercellular substance and imbedded in a tough gelatinous matrix, as **ascococci.**

II. The Bacillus.

Morphology.—The bacilli or rod-shaped (desmo-) bacteria are distinguished by the fact that their two longest sides are parallel to each other; the two short sides being at times straight, at others concave, and at others again convex.

Varieties.—They are said to be (1) **slender** when their breadth is to their length as 1 to 4 or more, and (2) **thick** when it is as 1 to 2. They **develop singly** or **in pairs** or in **long threads** or **filaments**, being attached together always by their narrow ends.

III. The Spirillum.

The spirilla or curved or spiral bacteria **develop** either **singly** or **in pairs** or **in long twisted** or **corkscrew filaments.**

The Variations in Development of Each Species.

Though under varied conditions of growth the form of any one species may vary considerably, yet these three main divisions under similar conditions are permanent—that is, micrococci always develop into micrococci, bacilli into bacilli, and spirilla into spirilla.

FIG. 2.

a. Staphylococci *b*. Streptococci. *c*. Diplococci. *d*. Tetrads. *e*. Sarcinæ. (Abbott.)

FIG. 3.

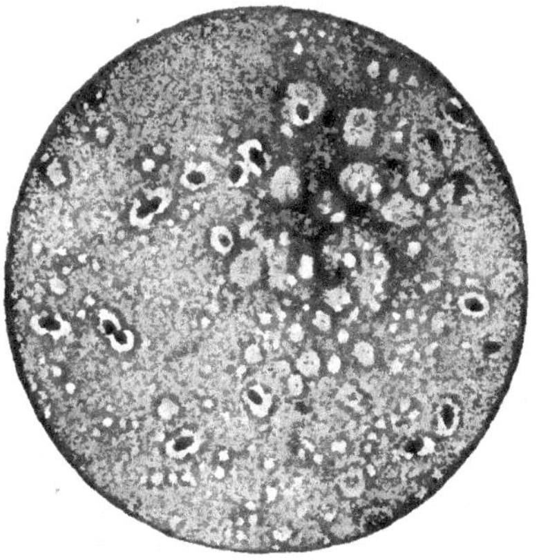

Diplococcus of pneumonia, with surrounding capsule. (Park.)

FIG. 4.

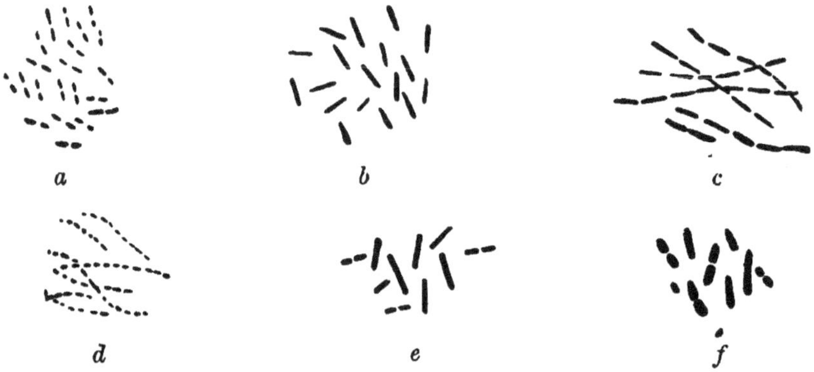

a. Bacilli in pairs. *b.* Single bacilli. *c* and *d.* Bacilli in threads. *e* and *f.* Bacilli of variable morphology. (Abbott.)

FIG. 5.

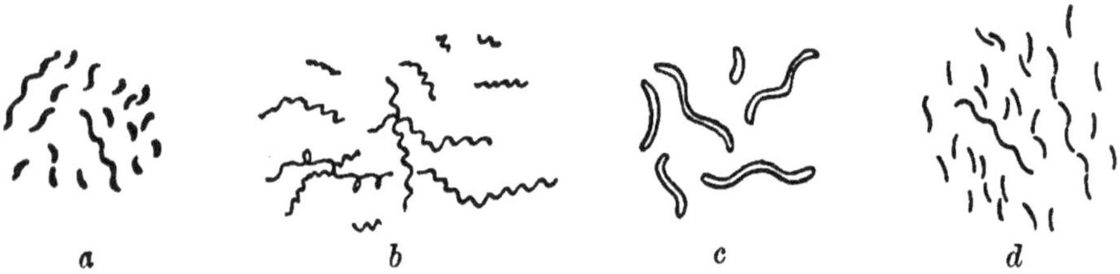

a and *d.* Spirilla in short segments and longer threads—the so-called comma forms and spirals. *b.* The forms known as spirochæta. *c.* The thick spirals sometimes known as vibrios. (Abbott.)

FIG. 6.

a. Spirillum of Asiatic cholera (comma bacillus); normal appearance in fresh cultures. *b.* Involution-forms of this organism as seen in old cultures. (Abbott.)

Occasionally under peculiar conditions what are known as **involution-forms** are produced, forms which may scarcely be recognized as those belonging to the original bacteria. These points are shown by Figs. 2, 3, 4, 5, 6.

THE SIZE OF BACTERIA.

Bacteria require to be seen and studied by the highest powers of the microscope; they vary in size from 0.2 to 30 mikrons. (A mikron is $\frac{1}{1000}$ millimeter; about $\frac{1}{25000}$ inch.) The **micrococci** have a diameter of from 0.2 to 1 mikron or more. **Bacilli** and **spirilla** vary in length from 2 to 30 mikrons or more; in breadth, from 1 to 4 mikrons. The average length of **pathogenic bacilli** is 3 mikrons.

THE REPRODUCTION OF BACTERIA.

As mentioned in the foregoing paragraphs, bacteria **multiply by fission.**

I. Fission.

In the case of **cocci,** the round or oval cells show a little indentation beginning in the membrane at two, four, or eight points of its periphery, according as the division is to occur in two, four, or eight parts; this indentation increases until the original cell is divided into hemispheres, quadrants, or octants, as the case may be. These parts remain attached to one another until complete spheric cocci are formed from each part, and they then separate or not according to the nature of the bacteria.

In some forms of **diplococci,** as the gonococci, complete spheres are never formed, the cells remaining attached to each other in pairs as hemispheres.

In the case of nearly all **bacilli** and **spirilla** the cells increase to nearly double their original size before division, and the *division always takes place in the direction of the length of the bacterium.* The daughter cell remains attached for a while to its parent cell after fission is complete; occasionally this attachment persists for a long time, so that large filaments consisting of a number of bacteria are formed.

II. Sporulation.

1. The Endospore.

Division by fission is the usual mode of the reproduction of bacteria, but at times, depending upon various circumstances to be mentioned later, what are known as **spores** are formed by a number of **bacilli and spirilla.** These spores, which are perhaps the **equivalents of seeds** for the higher plants, are formed in this way: in the body of the bacillus, generally at its centre, occasionally at one of its poles, a number of dark highly refractile granules accumulate, and are soon changed into an oval, glistening, highly refractile body which is surrounded by a membrane of the same composition as that of the cell itself, but thicker and more resistant. One spore only is formed in each cell. Sometimes the spore-formation causes no change in the shape of the rod. At other times there is a bulging of the centre of the body of the bacillus, where the spore is located, with a general tapering to the two ends, giving to the bacillus the shape of a *spindle.* This is called a **clostridium.** Again, when the spore is formed at one of the poles, there is sometimes a bulging of that part, giving to the bacillus the appearance of a *nail* or *drum-stick*, whence the name of **drummer-bacillus** for the cell. Fig. 7 shows these forms well.

FIG. 7.

a b c d

a. Bacillus subtilis with spores. *b. Bacillus anthracis* with spores. *c.* Clostridiumform with spores. *d.* Bacillus of tetanus with endospores. (Abbott.)

Soon after the formation of the spore the rest of the **body of the cell disintegrates** and breaks down, and the oval spore is liberated.

The spores are **characterized,** on account of their thick membrane, by resistance to external influences which would be fatal to the bacilli themselves, such, for instance, as *extremes of heat or cold, desiccation,* and the *action of chemicals;* also, to a great extent, **staining** by the penetration into their body of certain dyes which have great affinity for the protoplasm of ordinary bacteria, so that a special method must be adopted for their staining, as will be described later.

Spores therefore **preserve the species**, when these would be destroyed if dependent solely on the bacilli for their preservation.

2. The Arthrospore.

The foregoing spore-formation, known as **endospores**, is the usual mode of spore-formation found in bacteria, and is limited to the rod and spirilla forms; but another form of spore, called **arthrospore**, is mentioned by some as occurring occasionally in the round or cocci forms. This consists in a special jointed projection forming from the outside of the cells, and capable later of developing into the original cell. *This form of spore-formation is generally doubted at the present time.*

Spores are **incapable of producing other spores**, and can, only when placed in suitable conditions, develop into the type of bacilli which gave them birth. When this occurs the spore begins to elongate, loses its glistening appearance, and finally its membrane ruptures at one end or in the centre and gives exit to a fully developed bacillus.

Spores **may be distinguished** from rounded bacteria by means of their brighter, more glistening appearance, their power of resisting stains, and the fact that in suitable media they develop into bacilli.

Significance of Sporulation.—Whether the original idea that spores form, in bacteria capable of producing them, only when the latter are submitted to external noxious influences, and for the purpose of perpetuating the species, or whether, as more recently maintained, sporulation is the result of the highest expression of the complete development of bacteria, is not at present fully determined, though the dictum of authorities inclines to the latter view, and the spore-formation of some of the best-known and studied bacteria, as anthrax, seems to lend color to this theory.

THE MOTILITY OF BACTERIA.

Motility, or the **power of transporting themselves** from place to place, is possessed by a number of bacteria. This is **effected by** filamentous or hair-like processes arising from the body of the bacteria, and called **flagella.** It must not be confounded with the peculiar whirling or dancing movement so often seen under the microscope, even in inorganic particles, and called the **Brownian movements.** Motility, except in two instances, has so far been observed only in bacilli and spirilla. Its rapidity depends on the particular bacterium, its mode of cultivation, the age of the culture, and other similar factors. Some bacteria after repeated artificial cultivation seem to lose their motility, which, however, may be restored fully by passing through an animal.

FIG. 8.

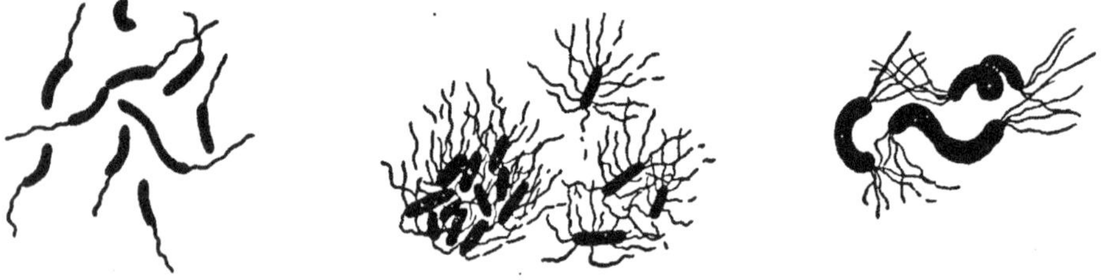

a b c

a. Spiral forms with a flagellum at only one end. *b.* Bacillus of typhoid fever with flagella given off from all sides. *c.* Large spirals from stagnant water with wisps of flagella at their ends (*Spirillum undula*). (Abbott.)

The **flagella** are hair-like processes consisting of the same material as the bacterial cell-membrane, and are so minute as scarcely to be visible under the highest power of the microscope unless they are stained by special processes, as will be described in the chapter on staining. Whenever there is only a single flagellum at one of the poles of the bacillus, this is said to be **monotrocha**; whenever there is a single flagellum at each pole of the bacterium, it is said to be **amphitrocha**; whenever there is a cluster of flagella at one pole, the bacterium is said to be **lophotrocha**; and finally, when a varying number of flagella seem to arise from different portions of the body of the bacterium, it is said to be **peritrocha.** These features are shown in Fig. 8.

THE RELATION OF OXYGEN TO BACTERIAL LIFE.

Bacteria are divided into **aërobic** and **anaërobic** according as they require oxygen or not for their development. Some thriving best in the presence of oxygen are able to develop, however, without the presence of this gas; these are called **facultative anaërobic.** Others thriving best without oxygen but able to develop in the presence of this gas are called **facultative aërobic.**

THE RELATION OF DEAD AND LIVING ORGANIC MATTER TO BACTERIA.

Bacteria are also divided into **saprophytes** and **parasites,** according as they require for their development merely the presence of decomposable organic matter or the body of a living higher organism, as host, on which they live. Should they also be able to live outside their host, they are called **facultative parasites.** The disease-producing germs are always parasitic.

THE ESSENTIAL CONDITIONS OF BACTERIAL GROWTH.

For the proper development of bacteria the following are required: heat, moisture, and the presence of some decomposable organic matter, with special chemical reaction of the culture-medium.

I. Heat.

A **temperature between 10° and 40° C.** is required for the development of **adult bacteria,** but the degree varies greatly according to the different species. Some of the **parasites** thrive best at a temperature in the neighborhood of that of the human body, about 36° or 37° C.; others, the **saprophytes,** seem to grow best at the ordinary room temperature, between 20° and 30° C.; some few again seem to be able to grow and multiply at a temperature near the freezing-point; and not long ago a number have been shown to develop abundantly at a temperature above 70° C. *As a general rule, however, a temperature of 0° C. and one above 60° C. are fatal* *within a few minutes for the ordinary non-spore-bearing bacteria.* **Spores** are able to **resist** for a long time the effects of cold and excessive heat. Some have developed after having been immersed for a long time in liquid air (temperature, —200° C.), and also after exposure to dry heat of above 150° F. for sixty minutes and moist heat for thirty or forty minutes.

II. Moisture.

A certain amount of moisture is absolutely indispensable for the growth of bacteria, desiccation being fatal within a few minutes for nearly all the **fully formed bacteria.**

Spores, however, are capable of developing after being kept dry for an indefinite period.

III. Decomposable Organic Material.

A certain amount of decomposable organic matter is **indispensable** for the development of the bacteria. This they **decompose into simple elements,** and are so able to obtain the nitrogen and carbon necessary for their sustenance. At the same time they **set free carbon dioxide** and **nitrogen** from the remainder, and so provide for the nourishment of the higher vegetables, which must have these substances free in order to support life. And in so doing bacteria render a service of incalculable value, as without it life in the animal kingdom would soon be extinct.

Different bacteria require a greater or lesser proportion of the proteid substances for their nutrition; and according as substances contain these in a more or less favorable condition for absorption they are said to be more or less good culture-soils or media.

Some few species seem to be able to **live in saline solution** and in other media where there is no appreciable amount of organic matter, but in these cases they probably obtain their nutrition from the decomposition of slight traces of ammonia and the carbon dioxide of the air contained in the water.

Again, some bacteria seem to have the **power of decomposing**

ammonia and **building up nitrite** and **nitrate compounds**; these are known as the **nitrifying bacteria**, and as a class are important, and are being carefully studied.

IV. Special Chemical Reaction of the Culture-medium.

Bacteria are likewise profoundly influenced in their growth by the reaction of the medium in which they grow, most bacteria requiring a **neutral** or **faintly alkaline medium**, some few a **faintly acid** one. This characteristic is found an element of danger for bacterial life: for the bacteria which require alkaline surroundings have, as a rule, the property of secreting acids, so that after a while they render the medium unfit for their own further growth long before the pabulum is exhausted.

THE INERT AND INHIBITIVE CONDITIONS OF BACTERIAL LIFE.

1. **Diffuse daylight** seems to have little or no influence on bacterial growth, but most bacteria and their spores are killed after a more or less prolonged exposure to the direct rays of the sun, a fact of great importance in practical hygiene.
2. **Electric currents** and the **X-rays** seem to have but little influence on bacterial growth.
3. **Compressed air** seems to retard the growth of bacteria.
4. A number of **chemical substances** either kill off bacteria or arrest their growth—as will be spoken of more fully under the head of Antiseptics and Disinfectants.

THE VITAL MANIFESTATIONS OR FUNCTIONS OF BACTERIA.

These are manifold and various, and occasionally attempts at classification have been based on some of these special functions.

1. **Fermentation.**—The **alcoholic** and **acetic acid fermentation** are the work of the yeast fungi; but the **butyric** and **lactic acid fermentation** in milk are caused by a number of bacteria,

the most prominent of which are those that bear the respective names. This class of bacteria are called the **zymogenic.**

2. **Putrefaction** is caused by a variety of bacteria called **saprogenic.**

3. **Pigments** and **colors** are produced by a number of bacteria called **chromogenic.** Sometimes the pigment is secreted by the cells and diffused in the surrounding media, the bacteria remaining uncolored. At other times the pigment is limited to the cell-protoplasm and membrane, the surrounding medium remaining uncolored. As a rule, these pigments are produced only in an atmosphere of oxygen.

4. Some bacteria, called **photogenic, phosphorescent,** or **fluorescent,** have the property of **emitting** and **producing light.**

5. Bacteria **secrete poisonous substances** which are sometimes highly deadly, and which from their character are classed as **ptomaines** and **toxalbumins.**

The *ptomaines* are crystallizable basic substances, *closely allied to the vegetable alkaloids.*

The *toxalbumins* are non-crystallizable substances, *similar to albumin* or *protein.*

It is by the poisonous effects of these toxins that most bacteria affect the human body.

6. Some bacteria **liquefy gelatin,** and this fact is made use of in differentiating the different species. This liquefaction has been demonstrated to be **caused by a soluble peptonizing ferment** secreted by the bacteria cells, and after filtration of a bouillon culture of the liquefying bacterium the filtrate free from bacteria possesses the same power of liquefying gelatin.

7. Some bacteria **produce acids** and other **alkalies**—as may be demonstrated by their action.

8. **Various gases,** such as carbon dioxide, marsh gas, hydrogen sulphide, etc., are the products in some instances of bacterial growth.

9. A number of bacteria **produce odors** without the apparent production of gases.

10. A few **produce aromatics,** and are used extensively in the arts.

11. Again, a certain class **peptonize milk** by means of

enzymes which they secrete. Some cause a reduction of the nitrites.

12. Others **oxidize nitrogen** into nitrites, and even nitrates.

13. Finally, some bacteria **cause disease in man and animals.** These, called **pathogenic,** are of the greatest interest to physicians, and it is the discovery of this pathogenic property which in the last twenty years has given such an impetus to the study of bacteriology.

QUESTIONS.

Who first discovered microörganisms in decaying vegetable infusions?

To what kingdom were they thought to belong at first?

What classification is generally accepted at present?

Name the three varieties of fungi. What criticism may be made of this classification?

Give a proper definition of bacteria.

Of what does the bacteria cell consist?

What causes some bacteria to have a capsule? Are the capsules generally retained by bacteria when grown artificially?

What causes some bacteria to be more difficult of staining than others?

Into what three varieties or species are bacteria divided?

What are megacocci? Micrococci? Diplococci? Merismopedia? Sarcinæ? Streptococci? Staphylococci? Ascococci?

What is the shape of bacilli? When are they said to be slender? When thick? How do they develop? What are spirilla? Can one species develop into another species?

What are the limits of size of bacteria?

What is a mikron?

What is the average length of the pathogenic bacteria?

How do bacteria multiply? Describe this process in the case of cocci, bacilli, and spirilla?

What are spores, and how are they formed?

How do spores compare with bacteria in their power of resisting injurious external influences and of staining? To what is this due?

What is meant by a clostridium?

What is meant by a drummer-bacillus?

What is the name of the ordinary spores?

What is meant by arthrospores?

What is the theory of spore-formation?

What is meant by motility, and what species have this power?

What are flagella?

What names are given to bacteria according to the position and number of their flagella?

What is meant by aërobic bacteria? Anaërobic? Facultative aërobic? Facultative anaërobic?

What are saprophytes? Parasites?

What conditions are required for the proper development of bacteria?

What is the most favorable temperature for bacterial growth?

What is the effect of cold? Of excessive heat?

How do spores differ from bacteria in their reaction to heat and cold?

What is the effect of moisture on bacterial life? Of desiccation?
What pabulum is necessary for the life of bacteria?
How do you explain the life of bacteria in saline solution and in media with no appreciable amount of organic matter?
What is meant by culture-soils or media?
What other conditions influence bacterial growth?
What is the effect of sun-light on bacteria? Of electric currents? X-rays? Of compressed air?
What are the manifold functions of bacteria? Enumerate and explain the same.
What is the chemical difference between a ptomaine and a toxalbumin?
What are zymogenic? Chromogenic? Photogenic? Pathogenic bacteria?

CHAPTER II.

THE EXAMINATION AND THE STAINING OF BACTERIA.

THE EXAMINATION OF BACTERIA.

For the purpose of examining bacteria the **highest power of the microscope** is necessary, although many are seen with an ordinary dry $\frac{1}{4}$ or $\frac{1}{6}$ objective. Ordinarily, however, the $\frac{1}{12}$ oil-immersion objective is indispensable for the proper study of microörganisms.

Bacteria are examined either alive and in their natural condition, or dried on microscope slides or cover-glasses as a thin film, and stained.

1. For the purpose of **examining bacteria in their natural condition,** it is only necessary, *when the bacteria are in liquid medium,* to put a droplet of the liquid on a slide, cover lightly with a thin cover-glass, put upon the stage of the microscope, and bring into focus the $\frac{1}{12}$ inch oil-immersion objective, being careful to close almost completely the iris diaphragm underneath the substage condenser.

When the bacteria are in solid medium, a minute particle of the culture is taken up on a sterilized platinum needle and stirred up in a small drop of sterilized water on a slide, and a cover-glass applied as above.

In these ways the **form, shape, mode of grouping,** and **motility** of the bacteria may be very well seen and carefully investigated.

The Hanging-drop Preparation.

When it is necessary to keep them under observation for some time, however, or when it is desired to study their **development, multiplication,** or **sporulation,** what is known as the hanging-drop preparation or culture is resorted to.

This **consists** in placing a small drop of the liquid containing the bacteria on a thin cover-glass and placing upon this cover-glass a slide with a concavity in its centre, known as the hanging-drop slide, after having carefully lubricated the edges of the surface around the concavity with vaselin, so that the slide will adhere to the cover-glass when it is pressed down on it. In this way a hermetically sealed, transparent, moist chamber is obtained, which may be kept under observation on the stage of a microscope almost indefinitely.

FIG. 9.

Longitudinal section of hollow ground glass slide for observing bacteria in hanging drops. (Abbott.)

2. The foregoing are very simple and useful methods for rapid examinations of bacteria, and have many applications, but they are far from satisfactory in all cases, as they fail to bring out full details of bacterial structure. For this purpose recourse must be had to the staining methods introduced by Koch, and perfected by Weigert, Loeffler, and many others. In this method bacteria are examined dead.

THE STAINING OF BACTERIA.

I. The General Mode of Procedure.

One or several droplets of the suspected liquid are spread *thinly* and *evenly* on the surface of a slide or thin cover-glass, or, in case of a solid, a small particle is diluted with sterile water and spread in the same way on the slide or cover-glass. This is allowed to dry in the air, protected from dust, or else is held in a suitable forceps high up over the flame of an alcohol lamp or Bunsen gas-burner until dry, thus forming a thin film on the surface of the glass. After this step has been carefully taken the slide or cover-glass is taken up with a pair of forceps and passed several times through the flame, *film-side up*, for one-half to one second at each pass, *three times in the case of a cover-glass* and *eight or ten passes in the case of a slide;* which is for the purpose of **setting the preparation**, or coagulating the albuminoids and fixing them to the glass so that they will not be easily washed away in the subsequent procedures.

After allowing the preparation to cool well, it is ready for the staining reagents.

II. The Most Commonly Used Stains.

The basic anilin dyes, such as fuchsin, methylene-blue, gentian-violet or methyl-violet, and Bismarck-brown, are most commonly employed.

They are **made into saturated alcoholic solutions**, to be kept in stock, and are **freely diluted with water** whenever required for use.

III. The Application of the Dyes.

Nearly all the known bacteria, with the exceptions to be mentioned later, are readily stained by the watery solutions of any of the basic anilin dyes. The film on the slide or cover-glass, prepared as just described, is covered by a few drops of the stain, or the cover glass, *film-side down*, is floated in a watch-glass full of the staining solution; at the end of from one-half to two or three minutes the staining fluid is poured off, the slide or cover-glass washed rapidly in water and then allowed to *air-dry;* after which, in the case of cover-glass preparations, they are inverted upon a drop of Canada balsam on a slide and examined with the oil-immersion lens; or, when slides have been prepared, after washing and drying a drop of cedar oil is put over the preparation, and the same is examined with the oil-immersion objective without the use of a cover-glass.

Air-bubbles are often caught between the balsam and the cover-glass. Gentle uniform pressure begun at the centre of the cover-glass and progressively applied toward its periphery will ordinarily remove them. If this should fail, heat carefully applied until the balsam is quite soft will aid in the riddance of the others.

IV. The Special Methods of Staining.

As stated above, this method may be applied for the staining of nearly all bacteria. Some, however, are not so easily stained, and special methods must be resorted to to increase the penetrating power of the dye. The most commonly used will be here described.

1. Loeffler's Method.

In this method, instead of using the ordinary watery solution of an anilin dye, **Loeffler's alkaline solution of methylene-blue** is used. This is **prepared** as follows:

Concentrated alcoholic solution of methylene-blue,	30 parts;
Caustic potash solution (1 : 10,000),	100 " .

Mix well and filter.

This method stains well all the ordinary bacteria, but is specially useful for the **staining of the bacillus of diphtheria.**

2. Koch-Ehrlich's Method.

Anilin water is prepared by adding a few drops of anilin oil, drop by drop, to distilled water in a test-tube, shaking well after the addition of each drop and until the liquid assumes a milky appearance, after which it is filtered through moistened filter-paper until the filtrate is absolutely clear.

To 100 parts of this clear filtrate of anilin water, 10 parts of absolute alcohol and 10 parts of an **alcoholic solution of fuchsin, methylene-blue,** or **gentian-violet,** are added, and the whole thoroughly mixed and filtered. The preparation is better when made fresh in small quantity at each time it is needed, as it decomposes in a few days.

In Koch-Ehrlich's method this anilin water (violet, blue, or red) is used instead of the simple watery solution of the dye. It possesses **much more penetrating power,** and this again may be increased by gently heating the slide or cover-glass, over a Bunsen burner, while it is being stained.

It is **applicable** whenever it is desirable so to fix the color in the bacteria that one may by means of decolorizing agents remove the color from the surrounding objects and tissue and fix it solely on the bacteria themselves. Some bacteria so retain the color by this method that it serves to distinguish them from others which they very much resemble, but which do not possess the same persistent retention of the stain.

The **usual decolorizing agent** employed is either ordinary alcohol or diluted sulphuric or hydrochloric acid (1 : 4).

3. Gram's Method.

Treat the object to be colored with **anilin-water gentian-violet** for about three minutes, after which immerse in **Gram's fluid.** This **consists** of:

Iodine,	1 part;
Iodide of potassium,	2 parts;
Water,	300 " .

Maintain this immersion for five minutes, then pass the preparation through alcohol and rinse in water. If the object is still of a violet color, treat it again with Gram's fluid and alcohol *until no violet is visible to the naked eye.* This method is **applicable** to a number of bacteria, and serves as a mode of differentiation between some of them which could not otherwise be distinguished under the microscope. It serves also to color the capsule of bacteria, and, slightly modified, is useful for the stain of bacteria in tissue. A **contrast-color** should be given to the uncolored parts.

4. Ziehl's Carbol-fuchsin Method.

Make a **solution of carbol-fuchsin** as follows:

Fuchsin,	1 part;
Crystallized carbolic acid,	5 parts;
Alcohol,	10 " ;
Water,	100 " .

Immerse the glass in or cover same with the carbol-fuchsin solution, heat gently over the flame of a Bunsen burner, gradually bringing to a point *just below boiling;* repeat this two or three times; after which immerse in **nitric acid solution** (1 part of acid to 3 parts of water) *until the color is scarcely visible to the naked eye.* To ascertain this, wash off the acid from the film with water. If color is still faintly visible, remove it by dipping into alcohol; wash in water, dry, mount in Canada balsam, and examine. A **contrast-color** may be given to the rest of the specimen by employing **methylene-blue.**

This is a **useful** method in coloring cover-glass preparations for **tubercle bacilli** or for the **Bacillus lepræ.**

5. Gabbett's Method.

This is a **modification of Ziehl's method,** and is perhaps the best method, on account of its simplicity and rapidity, for the staining of the tubercle bacillus in secretions. It is as follows: Prepare a slide or cover-glass film as indicated, immerse in **Ziehl's carbol-fuchsin solution** for ten minutes, remove to **Gabbett's sulphuric acid methylene-blue solution** for three to five minutes, rinse in water, dry, mount, examine. *The tubercle bacilli are colored red and the other bacteria and cell-nuclei are colored blue.*

Gabbett's solution consists of:

Methylene-blue,	1 to 2 parts;
Sulphuric acid,	25 " ;
Water,	75 " .

Besides the foregoing means, which will stain the bacteria in films, bacteriologists adopt **special methods for the staining of bacteria in tissues**, and **for the staining of spores, flagella, and the capsules of bacteria.**

V. The Staining of Capsules.

1. Welch's Glacial Acetic Acid Method.

Prepare the cover-glass in the usual way. Cover the film with **glacial acetic acid**, pour off the acid immediately, do *not wash in water*, cover the film with **anilin-water gentian-violet solution** for three or four minutes, wash in a 0.5 to 2 per cent. **solution of sodium chloride**, dry, mount, and examine.

The *acetic acid coagulates the mucin of the capsules* and renders the same distinctly visible.

2. Johne's Method.

A cover-glass film prepared in the usual way is covered with a **solution of gentian-violet** and heated until steam rises. The stain is then washed off in water, and the cover-glass put into a **2 per cent. acetic acid solution** for from ten to fifteen seconds. It is again washed in water, dried, and mounted in balsam.

VI. The Staining of Spores.

Though with the ordinary method of staining, spores in bacteria may be recognized by their highly refractive appearance and by the fact that they have not taken the color, they may be stained themselves, however, by special methods.

The First Method (Abbott's).

A cover-glass preparation is covered with **Loeffler's alkaline methylene-blue solution** and held by its edge with forceps over the Bunsen burner flame until the fluid begins to boil. It is then removed from the flame, and after a few seconds heated again. This step is repeated a number of times for one or two minutes, after which it is washed in water, and **decolor-**

ized, until all blue coloring visible *to the naked eye* has disappeared, in the following solution:

Alcohol (80 per cent.),	98 parts;
Nitric acid,	2 " .

The cover-glass is then dipped for a few seconds into the following solution:

Saturated alcoholic solution of eosin,	10 parts;
Water,	90 " .

After this it is again rinsed in water, dried, and mounted.

The Second Method.

For Spores

Float a cover-glass preparation film-side down in a watch-glass full of **Koch-Ehrlich's fuchsin solution.** Take the watch-glass by its edge with a pair of forceps and hold same over a low Bunsen flame until the staining fluid begins to boil. Remove from the burner, and after a few minutes repeat this process five or six times. After cooling, the cover-glass, *without washing in water*, is transferred to a second watch-glass containing a **decolorizing solution** as follows:

Absolute alcohol,	100 parts;
Hydrochloric acid,	3 " .

Place the cover-glass, *film-side up*, at the bottom of this watch-glass and let it remain for one or two minutes. Remove, wash in water, stain with **methylene-blue solution** for one or two minutes, wash rapidly in water, dry, and mount.

By this method the spores will be stained red and the body of the bacteria cells blue.

The Third Method.

Cover-glasses are prepared in the usual way. After fixing, the preparation is immersed in **chloroform** for two minutes, washed in water, placed for one or two minutes in a **5**

per cent. solution of chromic acid, again washed in water, and stained in hot **Ziehl's carbol-fuchsin solution** for five minutes. The staining fluid is poured off and, *without washing in water*, the preparation is **decolorized in 5 per cent. sulphuric acid.** After this it is again washed in water, and finally stained for two or three minutes in the **watery methylene-blue solution.**

The spores will be stained red, the body of the cells blue.

The action of the chloroform is to dissolve the fatty crystals that may be in the preparation. The chromic acid acts on the membrane of the spores and permits the entrance of the stain.

The Fourth Method (Fiocca's).

Ten to 20 parts of an **alkaline solution of an anilin color** are added to 20 c.c. of a **10 per cent. ammonia solution** in a watch-glass; then heat is applied until steam commences to be given off. The cover-glass stays in this hot solution from three to five minutes; it is then taken out and washed in a **20 per cent. solution of nitric** or **sulphuric acid** to decolorize it, then washed again, when a **contrast-color** may be given.

It must be remembered that there is considerable difference in the behavior of spores of different bacteria to the staining methods described; some stain very readily and others with considerable difficulty.

Practice will be the best guide as to which method is best to employ and to what extent it should be carried out.

VII. The Staining of Flagella.

The hair-like processes of the bacteria which serve for their locomotion, the *flagella*, can not, on account of their fineness, be seen in any stained specimen, nor can they be stained by any of the ordinary methods just described for staining bacteria. In order to make them visible, it is necessary to use special stains in which the action of **mordants** plays an essential part.

1. Loeffler's Method.

This is the most common method, and is as follows: Clean very carefully a thin cover-glass, and spread very thinly and evenly upon it as few as possible of the bacteria to be examined. *This is done by diluting with sterilized water a number of times the culture containing them.* The cover-glass is dried and fixed in the ordinary way. The following solution, known as a **mordant**, is then applied:

Tannic acid (20 per cent. solution in water, filtered),	10 parts;
Cold saturated solution of ferrous sulphate, filtered,	5 " ;
Saturated alcoholic solution of fuchsin,	1 part.

+ 1% NaOH OR 1/2% H_2SO_4

A few drops of it are placed on the film, and the cover-glass taken up with a pair of forceps and held over the flame of a Bunsen burner until the solution begins to steam, but not allowing the boiling-point to be reached. It is next washed rapidly in water, and then in absolute alcohol. The bacteria are to be stained in **anilin-water fuchsin solution** in the ordinary way.

Practice has shown, however, that different bacteria behave differently when exposed to this staining, and Loeffler himself has modified it to meet these requirements. Having found that the **addition of an alkali** favors the staining of flagella in some of the bacteria, he has added to his stain **1 per cent. of sodium hydrate.** In other cases, having found that an **acid** helps to bring out the flagella, he has added to his stain a **solution of sulphuric acid in water** of such strength that 1 c.c. will neutralize 1 c.c. of the sodium hydrate solution.

The following bacteria **require an acid solution** added to the stain: *Bacillus pyocyaneus*, the spirillum of Asiatic cholera, *Spirillum rubrum*, *Spirillum concentricum*, *Spirillum Metchnikowi.*

The following bacteria **require an alkaline addition** to the staining solution: *Bacillus mesentericus*, *Micrococcus agilis*, *Bacillus typhosus*, *Bacillus subtilis*, bacillus of malignant œdema, *Bacillus anthracis symptomatici.*

In a general way one may say that bacteria that produce acid in the media in which they grow require the addition of an alkali to the mordant, and those which produce alkalies require the addition of an acid.

2. Bunge's Method.

Bunge's method, a **modification of Loeffler's method**, is as follows: Prepare a **saturated solution of tannin in water**, and also a **5 per cent. solution of sesquichloride of iron in distilled water**; to 3 parts of the tannin solution add 1 part of the iron solution. To 10 parts of such a mixture add 1 part of **concentrated watery solution of fuchsin**. *This mordant should never be used fresh, but only after it has been exposed to the air for several days.* The cover-glass, thoroughly cleaned, is covered over by this mordant for five minutes, after which it is slightly warmed. It is then washed, dried, and stained faintly with a little carbol-fuchsin.

3. Pitfield's Method.

The following solution is used as a **mordant**:

Tannic acid (10 per cent. solution, filtered),	10 parts;
Corrosive sublimate (saturated aqueous solution),	5 " ;
Alum (saturated aqueous solution),	5 " ;
Carbol-fuchsin,	5 " .

Let this stand, and pour off the clear fluid. This mordant will keep for one or two weeks.

The **staining fluid** is prepared as follows:

Alum (saturated aqueous solution),	10 parts;
Gentian-violet (saturated alcoholic solution),	2 " .

This stain is to be prepared fresh every second or third day.

The **modus operandi** is as follows: On an absolutely clean cover-glass make a thin film as already described. Treat the film with the mordant applied cold for twenty-four hours, or with the mordant applied steaming, but not boiling, for three minutes; wash off thoroughly in water and dry; treat with the stain in the same manner as with the mordant; wash in water, dry, mount, and examine with an oil-immersion lens.

Other methods, such as **Van Ermengem's, Bowhill's,** etc., are highly recommended, but in the author's hands have given no better result than the foregoing three methods.

VIII. The Staining of Bacteria in Tissues.

1. The Staining of Sections.

Sections should be cut in the ordinary way in paraffin or celloidin. The sections are first put into water for a few minutes, then transferred to watch-glasses containing **watery solutions of any basic anilin dye,** and allowed to remain from five to ten minutes; they are next removed, rinsed in water, decolorized in a **0.1 solution of acetic acid** for a few seconds, again washed in water, then for a few minutes in absolute alcohol, and placed in cedar oil or xylol. They are allowed to remain in xylol from one-half to one minute. They are finally spread thinly on a spatula and brought to the slides, where the excess of fluid is taken up with blotting-paper; after which a drop of xylol balsam is placed on the sections, which are covered by thin clean cover-glasses, when they are ready for examination.

2. Gram's Method for Staining Bacteria in Tissue.

This is practically the same as the method for cover-glass preparations.

The section is stained in **anilin-water gentian-violet (Koch-Ehrlich)** diluted with one-third its volume of water. The section remains in this for about ten minutes at the temperature of the incubator. From this it is taken out and washed alternately in **Gram's iodine solution** and **alcohol** until all the naked-eye color has been extracted. It is then put into a **watery solution of eosin** or **Bismarck-brown** for one minute, again washed in alcohol a few seconds, and then put for one-quarter minute in absolute alcohol. After this it is transferred to xylol for one-half minute, then lifted to a slide, mounted in Canada balsam, and examined.

3. Weigert's Modification of Gram's Method.

Stain sections in the **Koch-Ehrlich anilin-water gentian-violet solution** for five or ten minutes; wash them afterward in water or **physiological salt solution.** Transfer to slide and remove excess of fluid with blotting-paper. Treat with the **iodine solution of Gram** for three minutes. Take up the excess of solution with blotting-paper. Cover the section with anilin oil, wash out the oil with xylol, and mount in xylol balsam. The anilin oil in this case acts as a decolorizing agent, and should be removed carefully, otherwise the specimen will not keep.

4. Kuehne's Carbolic Methylene-Blue Method.

Put the sections into the following solution for one-half hour:

Methylene-blue in substance,	$1\frac{1}{2}$ part;
Absolute alcohol,	10 parts.

Rub thoroughly in a mortar, and when the blue is completely dissolved add 100 parts of a **5 per cent. carbolic acid solution.** This solution should be made fresh when needed. The sections are stained for fifteen minutes in this solution and then washed in water until free from it. They are next transferred to a **2 per cent. hydrochloric acid solution,** then to a **solution of carbonate of lithium** (of the strength of 6 to 8 drops of a **concentrated watery solution** of the salt to 10 drops of water), and from this they are again washed in water and in absolute alcohol containing sufficient methylene-blue in substance to give it a blue color, then for a few minutes in anilin oil to which a little methylene-blue in substance has been added, and they are then rinsed out in pure anilin oil; from this they are placed in oil of turpentine or thymol for two minutes, then in xylol, and mounted in xylol balsam.

1st Stain 15 min wash 5th Aniline oil
2. 2% HCl to destain 6 Ol Thymol
3. Carb of Lithium 7 Xylol - +8

The **advantages of this method** are that it is generally applicable. Bacteria are not robbed of their color, and the tissue is sufficiently decolorized to render the bacteria visible and to admit of a contrast-stain.

5. Ziehl-Neelsen's Method.

The sections are warmed in a **solution of carbol-fuchsin** for one hour at a temperature of about 45° to 50° C., decolorized for a few seconds in a **5 per cent. sulphuric acid solution**, then put into **70 per cent. alcohol**, then in **absolute alcohol** for a few seconds to dehydrate, then in xylol to clear, and mounted on a slide in xylol balsam.

QUESTIONS.

What powers of the microscope are necessary for the examination of bacteria?

How are bacteria examined alive?

How is a hanging-drop preparation made?

What is the usual method of staining bacteria?

What are the most usual stains used for bacteria?

What is Loeffler's method?

Describe the Koch-Ehrlich method.

What are the usual decolorizing agents used?

What is Gram's method?

Describe Ziehl's carbol-fuchsin method.

Describe Gabbett's method.

Give Welch's method of staining the capsule of bacteria.

Give Johne's method.

Give Abbott's method of staining spores. Moeller's method. Fiocca's method.

Give Loeffler's method of staining flagella.

Which bacteria require the addition of acid to the mordant in order to stain their flagella? Which require the addition of alkalies?

Describe Bunge's method of staining flagella. Pitfield's method.

How would you stain bacteria in tissue? Give Gram's method. Weigert's method. Kuhne's method. Ziehl-Neelsen's method.

CHAPTER III.

THE PROCESS, MEDIA, AND UTENSILS OF THE CULTIVATION OF BACTERIA.

THE PROCESS OF THE CULTIVATION OF BACTERIA.

As mentioned before, bacteria **can not be separated** from one another **by form and appearance** under the microscope only. Indeed, in a number of instances, and even with the highest power of the microscope, some very inoffensive bacteria resemble very much and can not be differentiated from some that are highly pathogenic. Especially is this the case with the group of cocci.

In all such cases it is necessary to study the properties and mode of growth, and for this purpose the bacteriologist must use and prepare **suitable soils,** which are known by the name of **culture-media.** These culture-media must themselves be absolutely free from all live bacteria—that is, **sterile**; or, if they naturally contain bacteria, or if bacteria have been introduced during their preparation, these must be destroyed, or, in bacteriological language, the media must be **sterilized.**

THE MEDIA OF THE CULTIVATION OF BACTERIA.

All substances that **contain carbon and nitrogen compounds in assimilable form associated with water** may be used as culture-soils for bacteria. The culture-media used ordinarily are either **natural** or **artificial.** They may be **liquid** or **solid**; or, again, they may be **solid at the temperature used,** and **liquefied at a temperature not high enough to destroy bacterial life.**

I. The Most Commonly Used Liquid Culture-Media.

1. Milk.

Milk, as contained in the udders of the cow, is an excellent culture-medium, and is **generally sterile.** In its collection, however, it usually **becomes contaminated**—that is, bacteria are introduced into the milk: so much so that it is necessary to **sterilize** the same before using, and for this purpose what is known as the discontinuous or fractional sterilization by steam is resorted to.

Mode of Preparing Sterilized Milk.—Sterilized test-tubes from 5 to 7 inches in length, and about from 1 to 1½ inches in diameter, are filled to one-third their capacity with raw milk. The test-tubes are plugged tightly with ordinary cotton-batting, and are submitted to *live steam* in the steam sterilizer, at 100° C., for twenty minutes each time, on three consecutive days.

Before sterilization **tincture of blue litmus** may be added to the milk, and in this way the generation of acids by bacteria may easily be ascertained.

Milk prepared in the foregoing manner offers an **excellent culture-soil for** nearly all forms of bacteria; it serves also **for differentiating** between certain species accordingly as these have the property of coagulating the casein in the milk rapidly, slowly, or not at all.

2. Animal Blood-Serum.

Animal blood-serum obtained from a slaughter-house is an **exceedingly useful culture-medium.**

Its **mode of preparation** is as follows: In large cylindrical jars the fresh fluid blood is collected and allowed to remain untouched for a half-hour or an hour. After this, with a clean sterilized glass rod the coagulum that begins to form is detached from the sides of the vessel. The vessel then, well covered and protected from dust, is put into an ice-box, and at the end of twenty-four hours the clot, consisting of fibrin and of blood-corpuscles, is firm and sinks to the bottom of the vessel, leaving a clear serum above and around it. This **clear serum** may be siphoned or pipetted out and distributed among sterilized test-tubes, which, after being plugged with absorbent cotton-batting, are **sterilized in Koch's serum sterilizer** by the low temperature process to be described later.

Loeffler's modification of this method is generally used in all municipal laboratories for the cultivation and diagnosis of the bacillus of diphtheria;

Beef or mutton-blood is collected in the usual way, and to 8 parts of the clear serum 1 part of glucose-bouillon is added. This mixture distributed among test-tubes is sterilized and hardened in a slanting position in a steam sterilizer at a temperature between 80° and 90° C., for an hour each day during a whole week.

3. The **serum of ascitic fluid** and (4) the **fluid of hydrocele** are sometimes used for the cultivation of bacteria, and are prepared in the same manner as ordinary blood-serum.

5. Urine.

Urine may also be used for the cultivation of bacteria. For this purpose it is obtained by means of a sterilized catheter directly from the bladder, where it is generally sterile. It is safest, however, to sterilize it by steam for one hour before use.

6. Pasteur's Solution.

Filtered water,	100 parts;
Cane-sugar,	10 " ;
Ammonium tartrate,	1 part.

With the addition of 1 part of the ashes of yeast this was formerly extensively used as a culture-medium, but is now seldom used.

7. Bouillon.

(over)

Bouillon is the **most frequently used** of all the fluid media. It is **prepared** as follows: 1 pound of fresh lean beef is chopped up very fine and covered with 1 liter of *sterilized* water, and put into an ice-box for twenty-four hours, after which the aqueous extract is obtained by filtration through muslin by pressure, sufficient water being added if necessary to make up the original liter. To this filtrate 10 grams of peptone and 5 grams of sodium chloride are added, and the whole is cooked on a water-bath or in an enamelled iron kettle for a half-hour, after which sufficient of a saturated solution of sodium carbonate is added drop by drop to give the mixture a slight alkaline reaction. This, after cooking for fifteen or twenty minutes, is filtered through absorbent cotton several times into test-tubes and sterilized by steam for twenty minutes on three successive days.

The addition of 5 per cent. neutral glycerin to this bouillon makes an **excellent liquid culture-medium for tubercle bacilli,** and is highly recommended by Roux.

Any **standard beef-extract,** such as Liebig's, Armour's, Wyeth's, etc., may be used in making this bouillon, instead of the meat itself, 5 grams of the extract being added to 1 liter of water, the rest of the process being the same.

Peptone 10 gm NaCl 5 gm - $NaCO_3$ to alkaline reaction

II. The Most Commonly Used Solid Culture-Media.

1. Gelatin.

Nutrient gelatin is **prepared** as follows: A meat-infusion, as described for bouillon, is prepared and put into a large Bohemian flask of 2 liters capacity; to this meat-infusion are added:

Chloride of sodium,	5 grams;
Peptone,	10 " ;
Best quality gelatin	100 " .

The flask, loosely closed with a plug of absorbent cotton, is cooked over a water-bath until all the gelatin is dissolved. This will take from an hour and a half to two hours. After this the mixture, which will be found to be decidedly acid, is neutralized by means of a solution of sodium carbonate added drop by drop until the mixture is faintly alkaline, as in the bouillon. The flask is again put over the water-bath for an hour, after which the mixture is filtered hot through absorbent cotton and sterilized in the steam sterilizer for twenty minutes each day on three consecutive days.

Great care must be exercised to introduce the medium into the sterilizer only when steam is actively being generated, and not to allow it to cool in the sterilizer.

Advantages.—Gelatin is a **most excellent medium,** and remains **solid at room temperature** (22° or 24° C.), but is **readily liquefied** when exposed to a higher temperature.

Not only does it serve as an excellent medium for the cultivation of nearly all bacteria that grow out of the incubator temperature (36° to 37° C.), but it offers by the **plate-method** one of the best culture-soils **for isolating** bacteria.

As some of the bacteria **liquefy gelatin** and others do not, it is useful also in the **differentiation of these species.** On account of its clearness, its easy preparation, and the other advantages mentioned above, it is one of the best culture-soils available.

The **disadvantages** lie chiefly in the fact that it liquefies at a much lower temperature than that of the incubator, and can not therefore be used for the cultivation of some pathogenic bacteria which grow only at blood temperature.

2. Agar.

Nutrient agar is **prepared** much in the same manner as gelatin, except that 20 or 30 grams of 2 or 3 per cent. agar are added, instead of the gelatin, to the meat-infusion, and the process of cooking must be much more prolonged (four to five hours), as the agar is much slower in dissolving. It is necessary also sometimes, after dissolving the agar and neutralizing the mixture, to add the white of one or two eggs in order to **clarify the solution** before filtration. This is done by removing the flask from the fire and allowing it to cool to a temperature below 70° C. **After clarification** the mixture is again cooked for one and one-half to two hours and filtered through absorbent cotton two or three times. This filtration is a much more difficult process than with gelatin, and must be carried on in the steam sterilizer. After filtration the agar is distributed among test-tubes for use, and is sterilized by the same procedure as nutrient gelatin.

Nutrient agar has a **melting-point** much higher than that of gelatin, about 42° C., so that it may be used for the cultivation of those bacteria which grow only at or best at the temperature of the human body. It possesses all the **advantages** of gelatin, but is not so clear and transparent, and is **not liquefied** by the secretions of any known bacteria. It is useful also for the isolation of bacteria by means of plate cultures.

The **disadvantages** of agar, when compared with gelatin, lie chiefly in the greater difficulty of its preparation, and especially of its filtration.

3. The **glycerin-agar culture is obtained** by adding 5 per cent. of neutral glycerin to nutrient agar before sterilization. This makes a very favorable medium for the cultivation of the tubercle bacillus and of some other pathogenic bacteria.

4. A **mixture of agar and gelatin in bouillon** is sometimes used so as to obtain the advantages of the two substances combined. This mixture is **prepared** from bouillon in the usual way by dissolving in the bouillon 0.75 per cent. of agar and 5 per cent. of gelatin in the manner outlined in the foregoing paragraphs.

There are a number of **special filtering apparatus** constructed for the purpose of facilitating the filtration of agar. None in the author's estimation has any advantages over filtration through absorbent cotton in the steam sterilizer.

5. Potato Culture.

Koch called attention to the great **value** of potato cultures for **differentiating species of bacteria.**

The **mode of preparing** potatoes is as follows: A sound potato, of good size, with an intact epidermis, is chosen, and thoroughly washed and scrubbed with a brush to remove all dirt; after which, with a sharp-pointed knife, all the eyes and discolored parts are cut out of the potato. It is then washed again in water and put into a **solution of 1:500 bichloride of mercury** for an hour, after which it is cooked in the steam sterilizer for forty minutes on each of two successive days. Just before inoculation the potato is split into halves by means of a sterilized knife and allowed to fall into a moist chamber cut surface up.

The **moist chamber consists** of a double glass dish, the upper one of which is larger than the lower. This chamber should be thoroughly rinsed with a 1:500 solution of bichloride of mercury before use.

Some **precautions** are necessary to prevent contamination of the potato from external germs. The hand that cuts the potato should be thoroughly sterilized in a 1 : 1000 bichloride of mercury bath. It is better also after washing the potato and before submitting it to the bichloride bath to wrap it in some thin tissue paper, and to keep it in this paper until ready for inoculation.

Preparation of a Potato for Test-tube Culture.—By means of a cork-borer (Fig. 10) a cylinder is cut from a sound potato. This cylinder is cut *obliquely* into two pieces, and each placed into a large test-tube (Fig. 11), in which it is sterilized and cooked on three successive days for a half-hour in a steam sterilizer.

FIG. 10.

Nest of cork-borers, used to cut potatoes for test-tube cultures.

FIG. 11.

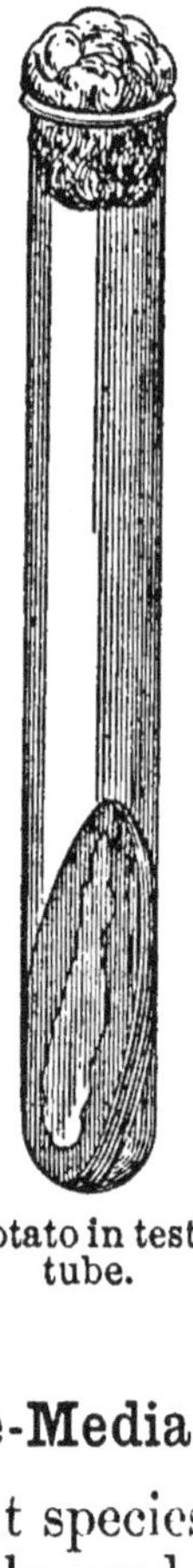

Potato in test-tube.

6. **Potato-paste** is sometimes used for cultivation. For this purpose a potato is boiled, peeled, and mashed with a little sterilized water, placed in a suitable glass dish, and sterilized for one-half hour on three successive days in a steam sterilizer.

7. **Bread-paste** is a useful medium for the growth of moulds, and is made in the same way as potato-paste.

III. The Most Commonly Used Special Culture-Media.

In making final distinctions between the different species of bacteria the following special media are occasionally used :

1. The Peptone Solution.

Dry peptone,	1 part;
Sodium chloride,	½ " ;
Distilled water,	100 parts.

This is filtered, decanted into test-tubes, and sterilized in the steam sterilizer.

This preparation is **chiefly used** for determining whether the bacteria secrete indol or not. It is necessary therefore to see that the peptone preparation used be chemically pure, also that the solution be free from the presence of carbohydrates.

2. **Glucose-, lactose-,** and **saccharose-bouillon.** These are **made** by adding to the bouillon after filtration and before sterilization from 1 to 2 per cent. of the desired kind of sugar.

THE UTENSILS OF THE CULTIVATION OF BACTERIA.

For **making** and **keeping** cultures the following **instruments, glassware,** and **utensils** are required :

1. **Perfectly clean glass tubes,** 5 to 7 inches long and ½ to

FIG. 12.

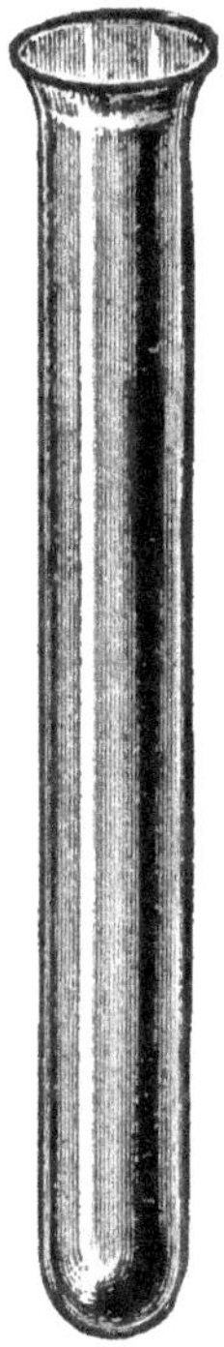

Glass test-tube.

FIG. 13.

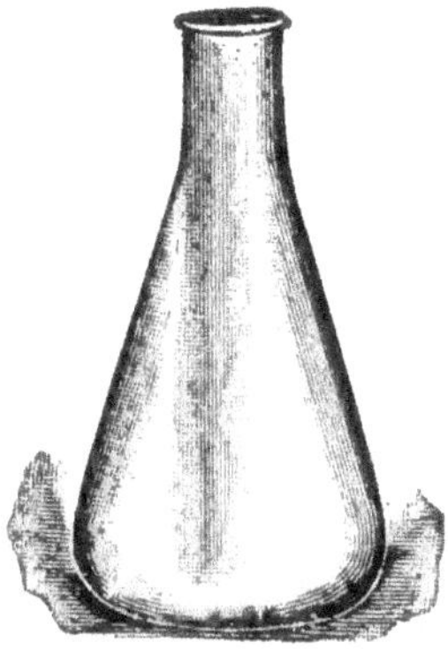

Erlenmeyer flask.

1½ inches in diameter (Fig. 12). These should be plugged with ordinary cotton-batting.

2. **Erlenmeyer flasks** (Fig. 13).

3. **Cylindrical brushes** with reed handle, and wire-handled brush of Lentz & Sons, for the purpose of cleaning test-tubes (Fig. 14).

FIG. 14.

a

b

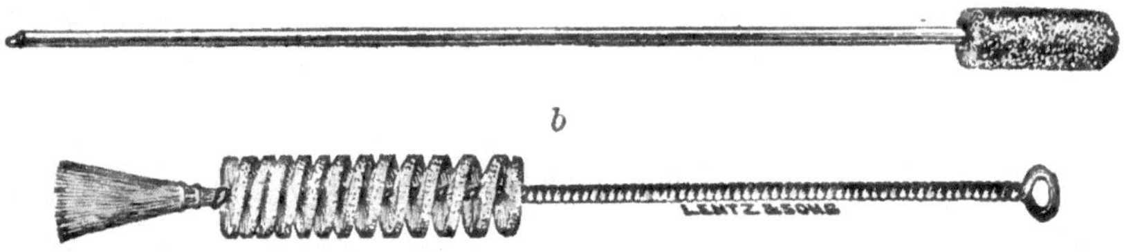

Brushes for cleaning test-tubes: *a*, with reed handle; *b*, with wire handle.

4. **Bohemian glass flasks** of 1 and 2 liters capacity.

5. **Platinum needles, straight** and **looped,** mounted in glass rods (Fig. 15).

FIG. 15.

a

b

(*a*) Looped and (*b*) straight platinum wires in glass handles.

6. **Plates of ordinary glass** about 4 by 5 inches, and **Russia iron boxes** to hold them during sterilization (Fig. 16).

FIG. 16.

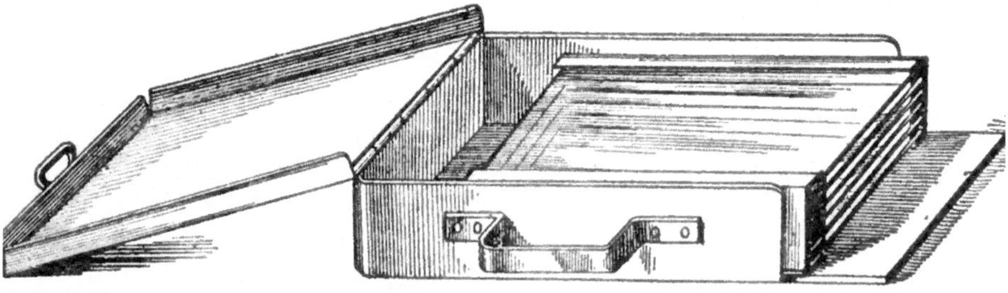

Russia iron box for holding plates, etc., during sterilization in dry heat. (Abbott.)

7. **Glass benches** for supporting plates (Fig. 17).

FIG. 17.

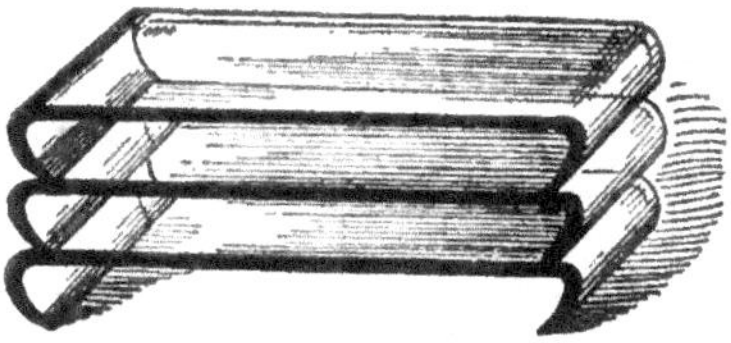

Glass benches for supporting plates.

8. **Graduated measuring cylinders** of 100 and 1000 c.c. capacity (Fig. 18).

9. **Graduated pipettes** of 1 c.c. capacity divided into tenths, and 10 c.c. divided into c.c. (Fig. 19).

FIG. 18.

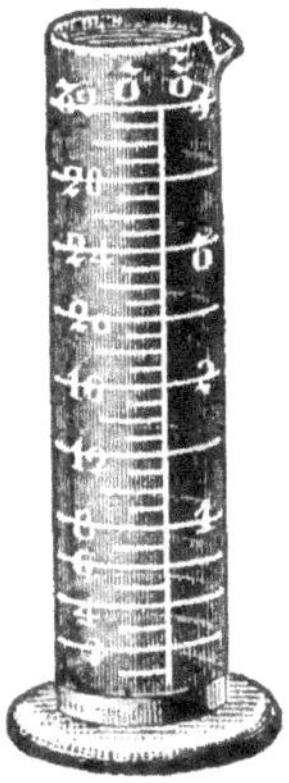

Measuring cylinder.

FIG. 19.

Graduated pipette.

FIG. 20.

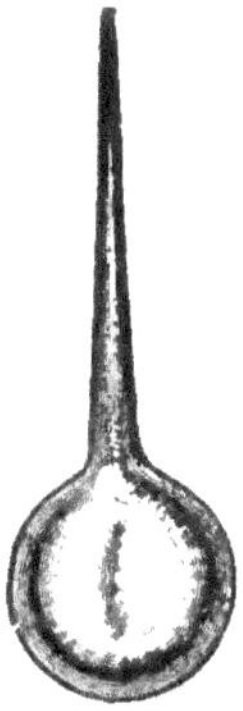

Sternberg bulb.

FIG. 21.

Bulb-pipette.

10. **Sternberg bulbs** (Fig. 20).

11. **Bulb-pipettes** (Fig. 21).

12. **Petri's double dishes** (Fig. 22).

FIG. 22.

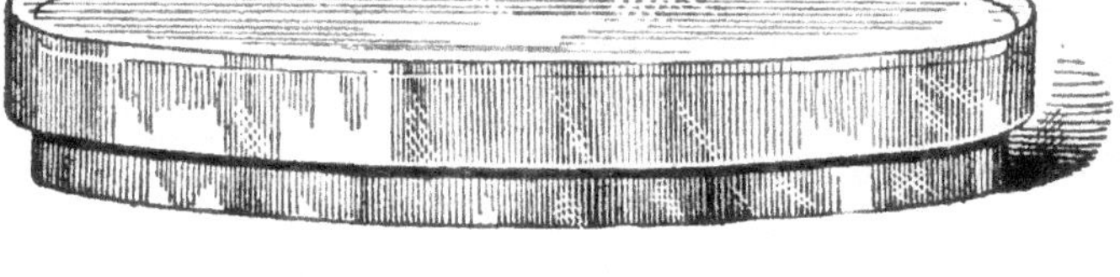

Petri's double dish, now generally used instead of plates. (Abbott.)

Fig. 23.

Moist chamber with a knob on the upper dish.

Fig. 24.

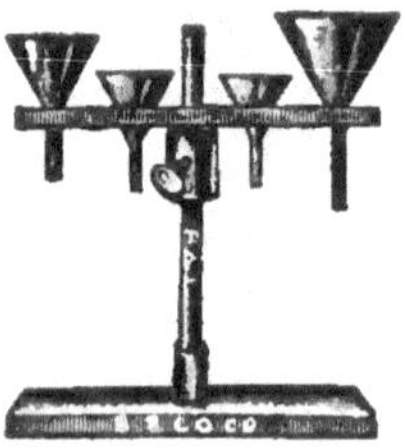

Wooden filter-stand.

Fig. 25.

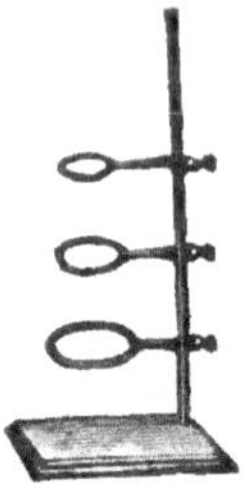

Iron stand with rings.

Fig. 26.

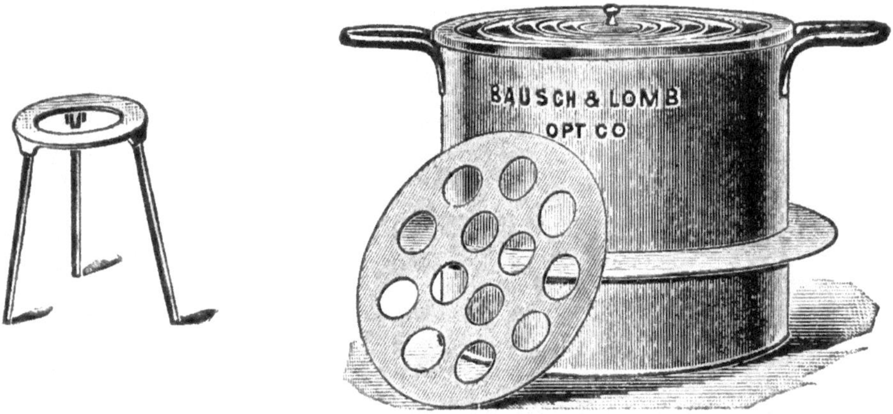

Iron tripod with water-bath.

Fig. 27.

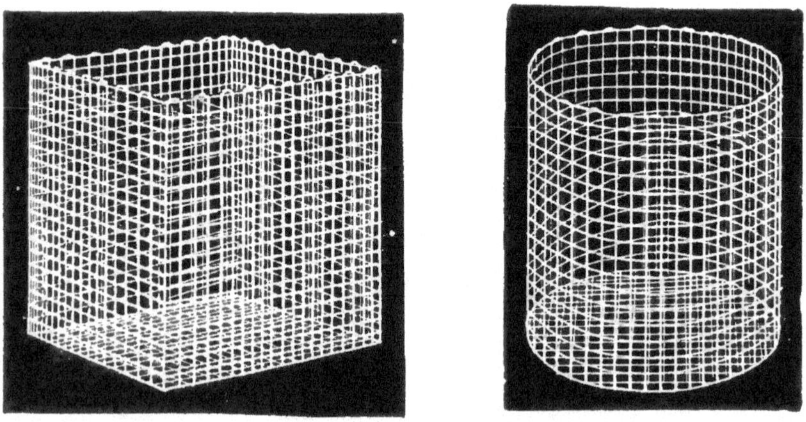

Wire baskets.

FIG. 28.

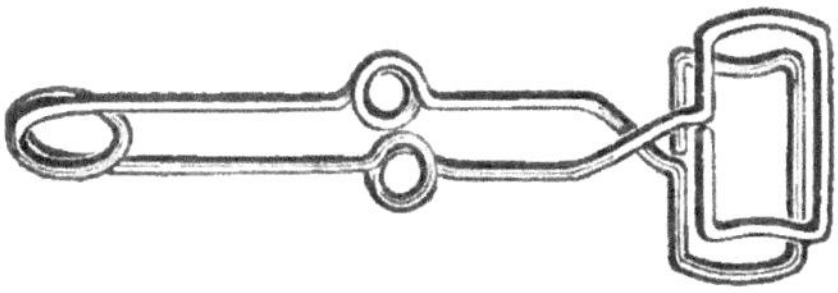

Pinchcock.

13. **Moist chambers** for potato and plate cultures (Fig. 23).
14. **Glass funnels** of different sizes, 1, 4, and 8 ounces.
15. **Wooden filter-stands** (Fig. 24).

FIG. 29.

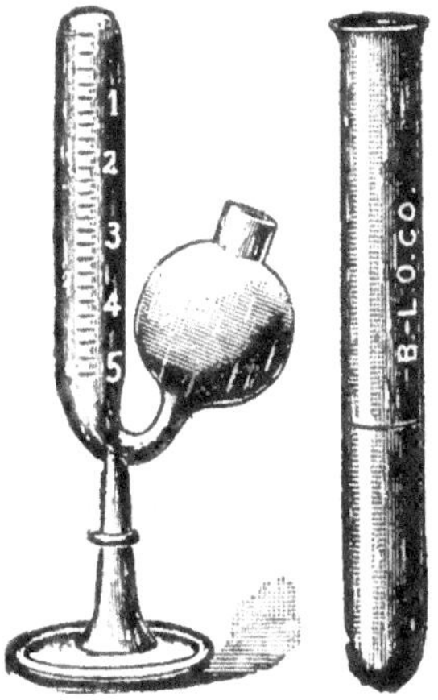

Fermentation-tube on left side; ordinary tube on right side.

FIG. 30.

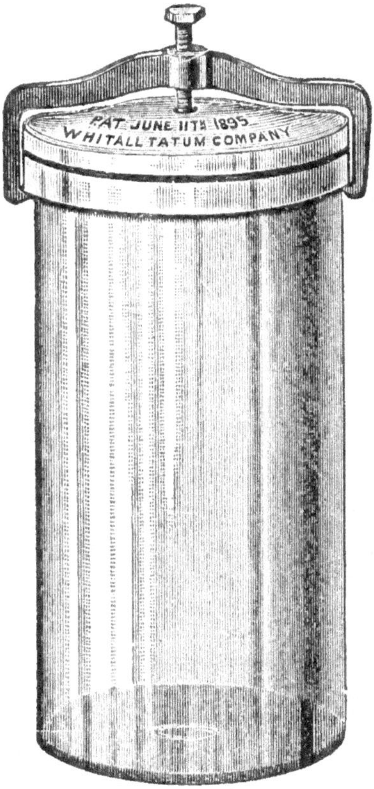

Anatomical jar for collecting blood.

16. **Iron stands with rings and clamps** (Fig. 25).
17. **Iron tripods with water-baths** (Fig. 26).
18. **Test-tube racks** of any standard design.

19. **Square and round iron wire baskets** for sterilizing test-tubes (Fig. 27).
20. **Perforated tin buckets** for sterilizing potatoes.
21. **Pinchcocks** (Fig. 28) for holding test-tubes.
22. **Fermentation-tubes** (Fig. 29).

FIG. 31.

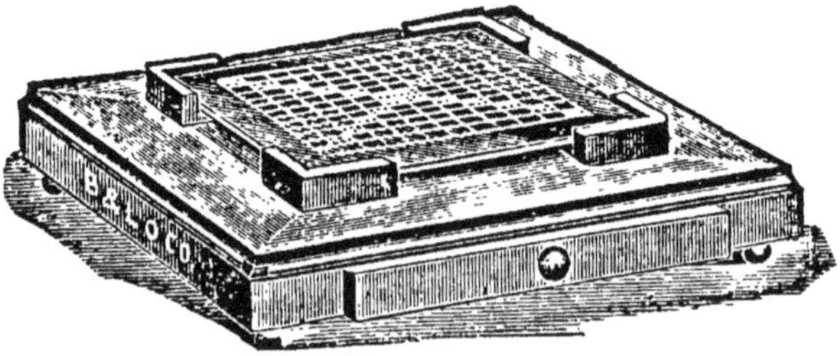

Wolfhuegel's ruled plate for counting colonies.

23. **A 2- and a 4-liter anatomical jar,** with tightly fitting cover, for the collection of blood-serum (Fig. 30).
24. **Wolfhuegel's ruled plates** for counting colonies (Fig. 31).
25. **Bunsen burners** of different sizes.

QUESTIONS.

What is meant by a culture-medium?
What is meant by the sterilization of culture-media?
How is milk prepared as a culture-medium?
How is milk sterilized when used for a medium?
Why is tincture of litmus added to milk medium?
How does milk help in differentiating between different species of bacteria?
What is the process of making blood-serum?
How is blood-serum sterilized?
What is Loeffler's modification of the blood-serum method?
What other animal fluids are occasionally used as culture-media?
What does Pasteur's solution consist of?
How would you prepare bouillon for cultures?
What are the principal solid cultures?
How would you prepare a nutrient gelatin?
How is nutrient gelatin sterilized?
What are the advantages of using gelatin as a culture? What are its disadvantages?
How would you prepare nutrient agar? What is difficult in the preparation of it? How would you sterilize it? What are its advantages and disadvantages when compared to gelatin?
How is agar-glycerin made?
How is agar-gelatin made?
What is the best way to filtrate agar?

Give Koch's method of preparing potatoes for a culture? What are the precautions necessary for protecting the potato from external germs?
How would you prepare a potato test-tube culture?
How would you prepare Dunham's solution?
How are glucose-, lactose-, and saccharose-bouillon prepared?

CHAPTER IV.

THE INOCULATION OF CULTURE-MEDIA WITH BACTERIA.

THE METHOD OF INOCULATING FLUID MEDIA.

For the purpose of cultivating bacteria in **liquid media** it is only necessary to **introduce the smallest possible particle containing the bacteria**, into the media, by means of a sterilized platinum needle (Fig. 15). For this procedure the culture-tube is held slightly inclined between the thumb and fingers of the left hand, its cotton plug removed by a twisting motion and placed between the *backs* of the third and fourth fingers of this hand, *being careful not to touch that portion of the cotton which fits inside of the tube.* The inoculating needle is rapidly introduced into the liquid and gently stirred around, after which the cotton plug is replaced, and the platinum needle sterilized by heating to redness in the flame.

It is good practice to accustom one's self never to take up a platinum needle, whether it is known to be inoculated or uninoculated, without first sterilizing it by heating it to redness in the flame, and allowing it to cool for a few seconds before taking up with it the inoculating material. The bacteria might otherwise be destroyed by the heat. Again, after use the needle should always be sterilized in the same manner before putting it down.

THE METHODS OF INOCULATING SOLID MEDIA.

1. For the inoculation of **potatoes** and **other solid media** not hereafter mentioned, it is only necessary to streak the surface of the medium with a platinum needle or other instrument which has been dipped into or which contains a small

fragment of the contaminating material, care having been taken beforehand to sterilize thoroughly the needle or instrument.

2. **Gelatin culture-tubes** are inoculated in one of three ways:

a. **Stab culture,** made by puncturing the centre of the solidified gelatin mass with a platinum needle previously charged with the bacteria.

b. **Slant cultures,** made by gently passing over the surface of the medium the inoculating needle; for this purpose the gelatin is made to solidify with the tube in an inclined position, so as to give a larger surface for inoculation.

c. **Plate cultures,** made by inoculating the gelatin mass, which has been previously liquefied by submitting it to a temperature of 30° C., with a platinum needle or loop as for liquid cultures, and pouring the liquid mass rapidly and evenly on a sterilized glass plate, allowing it to solidify well protected from dust.

The plate method, introduced by Koch, is **of great value** for the separation and isolation of bacteria. In this manner **each bacterium** introduced into the liquefied gelatin is fixed by the hardening of the gelatin and develops as a **separate colony,** the number of colonies being, as a rule, equal to the number of bacteria originally introduced.

Each colony grows in its own peculiar way, because each species has a definite way of growing in gelatin. This method therefore not only serves for the separation of the bacteria themselves, but also enables us to recognize one species from another. Indeed, the classical method of Koch for the separation and isolation of bacteria, though modified in some particulars, has not been essentially changed since its introduction. It is as follows:

Three sterilized gelatin culture-tubes about a third full and containing about 10 c.c. of the medium are liquefied by being submitted to a temperature of 30° C. Tube I. is inoculated with one or two loopfuls of the platinum needle from the contaminated substance, its cotton plug replaced, and the contents well shaken. After sterilizing the platinum needle one or two loopfuls from tube No. I. are introduced into tube

No. II.; both tubes are again plugged, and tube No. II. is in turn well shaken. The platinum needle is again sterilized, and finally one or two loopfuls from tube No. II. are introduced into Tube No. III., and the contents of the latter well stirred.

The three tubes are kept on a water-bath at a temperature of between 25° and 30° C., so as to keep the mass liquid. Meanwhile three sterilized glass plates are arranged on three cooling-stages, as depicted in Fig. 32. The gelatin from each

Fig. 32.

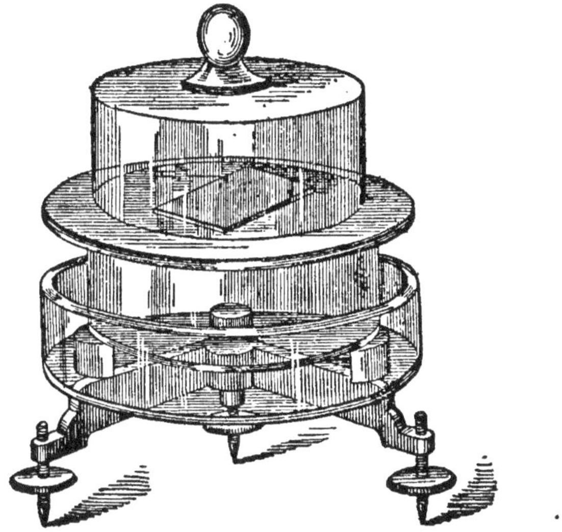

Levelling-tripod with glass cooling-chamber for plates.

of the tubes I., II., III. is slowly and evenly poured over the surface of the plates, correspondingly designated as No. I., II., III., and allowed to solidify. *It is necessary during the pouring and solidification of the gelatin on the plates that they be carefully protected by a cover against the dust and bacteria from without.*

After solidification is perfect the plates are transferred into culture-dishes placed on glass benches (Fig. 17), and properly labelled.

To harden the gelatin more rapidly, ice or iced water is generally kept in the lower dish of the cooling-stage. To insure

evenness of surface in the gelatin on the glass plates a **levelling-tripod** is used, as seen in Fig. 32. This tripod is easily set by means of a levelling glass.

Results.—In this manner each of the separate bacteria contained in the media will develop as separate colonies on the gelatin plates. Plate I., made from tube I., will contain a large number of bacteria; plate II. will contain the bacteria in much smaller number; and plate III. will contain only a few colonies, well separated; and in this way the characteristic growth of the separate colonies and their action on gelatin may be carefully followed out and studied. By this means also the observer may under a magnifying-glass with a fine sterile platinum needle pick out the individual colonies and inoculate fresh tubes, and so obtain pure cultures of any living organism.

3. **Plate cultures of agar** are made in the same way, but require more care in their preparation, as agar does not melt at a temperature below 42° C., and solidifies again at a temperature of 39° or 40° C., so that after inoculation in the liquid state the tubes must be kept in a water-bath between 40° and 42° C. until they are poured into the plates. The agar plates, however, may be incubated at blood temperature (37° C.), and the growth of bacteria noted.

In recent years **small double dishes**, known as **Petri's culture-dishes** (Fig. 22), have been introduced to take the place of the plates. For the inoculation, liquefied gelatin or agar is poured into the lower dish, and this is quickly covered by the upper dish. For this method no levelling apparatus and cooling-stage are required.

For **counting the colonies in the plates** the apparatus of Wolfhuegel (Fig. 31) has been adopted.

This consists of **regularly lined glass plates**, divided into squares and arranged as seen in the figure. By placing the culture-plate under the lined plate it is easy to ascertain the number of colonies contained in each of, for example, ten squares, and by a simple process of multiplication the number of colonies in the whole plate.

4. Instead of pouring out the liquid gelatin from the tubes

into plates after inoculation, Esmarch **rolls these tubes in a vertical position** until the gelatin is completely solid. This is hastened by rolling the tubes as shown in Fig. 33. By this excellent method there is less likelihood of contamination than by the plate method.

5. Gelatin and especially agar plates are occasionally made in a different way. The liquid medium is poured on glass plates and allowed to solidify before inoculation. When well hardened the **surface is streaked with the inoculating material**

FIG. 33.

Demonstrating Booker's method of rolling Esmarch tubes on a block of ice.

on a platinum needle. In this way the colonies grow along the streak much more superficially than they do in the ordinary plate method.

6. **Agar** and **blood-serum slant cultures** are made in the same manner as similar cultures on gelatin. They have one **advantage** over the gelatin culture by reason of being able to withstand the temperature of the incubator, 37° C.

THE CULTIVATION OF ANAEROBIC BACTERIA.

Exclusion of oxygen is absolutely necessary. For this purpose a number of methods have been suggested and used, some of which require special and elaborate apparatus. *All* *the foregoing methods of inoculation and cultivation are available only for the aërobic bacteria.*

1. **Cultivation of Tetanus Bacillus.**—The following method

Fig. 34.

Jar for anaërobic cultures.

Fig. 36.

Small incubator.

Fig. 35.

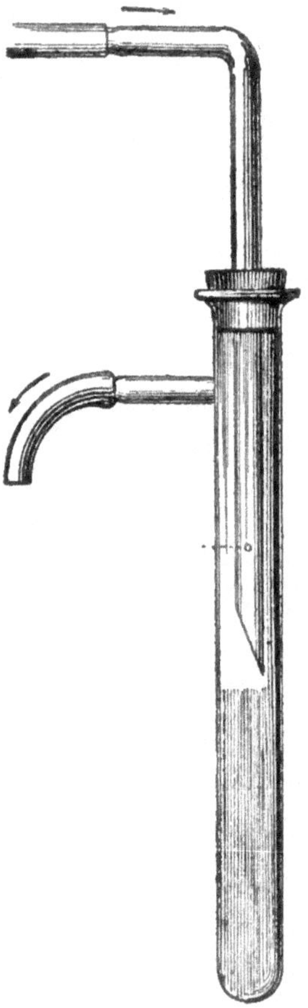

Mercurial thermo-regulator.

has been found very useful for the cultivation of this *strictly anaërobic* bacillus, aud answers all purposes in the author's opinion.

A culture-tube three-fourths full of the medium is heated to the boiling-point and allowed to cool to a temperature in the neighborhood of 40° C.; then a platinum needle charged

FIG. 37.

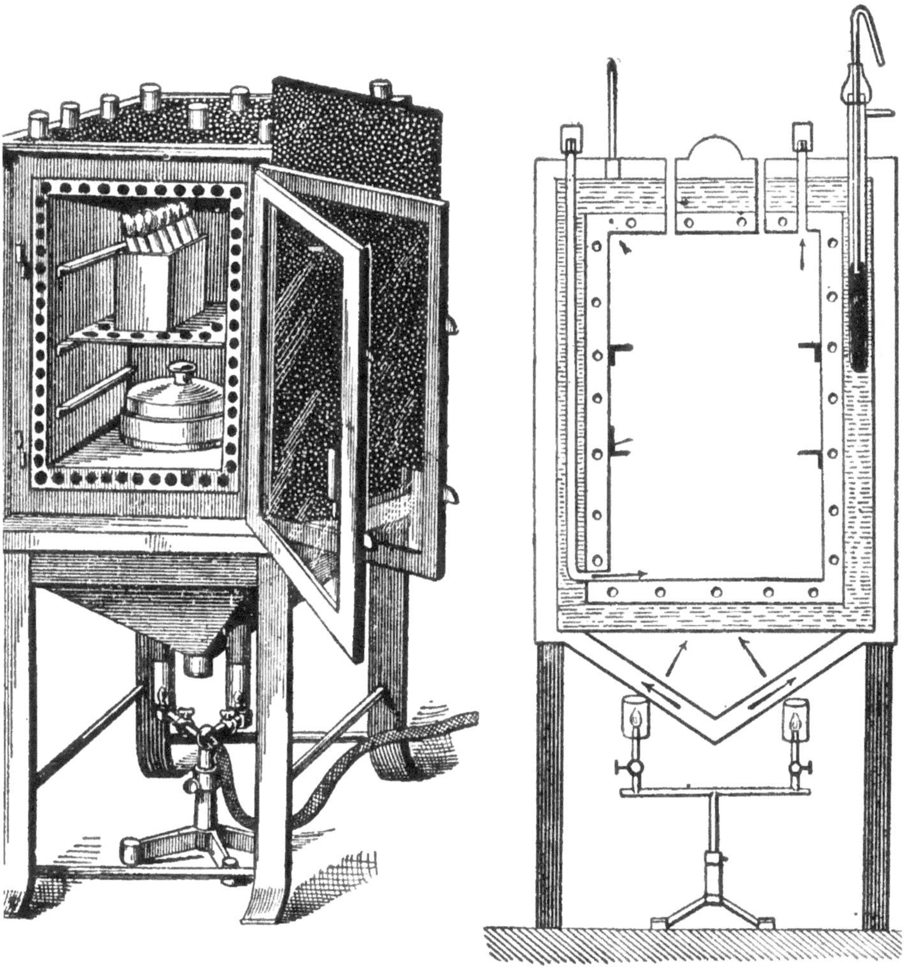

Incubator used in bacteriological work: *a* represents the incubator set up and containing a cage of tubes and a Petri dish; *b*, represents a vertical section of the incubator and displays the water-chamber, inner chamber, walls, vents, thermometer, valve, etc.

with the material for inoculation is dipped down to the bottom of the tube. With fluid media, immediately thereafter a layer of **paraffin oil** is poured on the surface of the liquid before introduction of the cotton plug. With **solid media,** the fluid is allowed to solidify after inoculation, and after solidification the **paraffin oil** is poured on the surface of the medium. *This effectually shuts out the oxygen, and as a rule allows a luxuriant growth of anaërobic bacteria.*

2. **Special apparatus, with oxygen replaced by hydrogen,** is also used for the cultivation of anaërobic bacteria.

The Incubator and The Thermostat.

For the purpose of growing bacteria it is often necessary or desirable to obtain a **constant temperature.** The **ordinary body-temperature,** 37° C., is the most favorable for the growth of the pathogenic bacteria. Apparatus especially constructed for maintaining a constant temperature are known as **incubators or thermostats.** They are **generally made of** double-walled metal, and contain water, which by means of a gas-jet at the bottom of the apparatus may be kept at a constant temperature (Fig. 37).

For **regulating the gas-supply** and to maintain the constant temperature, instruments known as **thermo-regulators** are used. A number of these are highly complicated, but for ordinary work is recommended **Reichert's** or **Dunham's mercurial thermo-regulator** (Fig. 35).

QUESTIONS.

How do you inoculate a fluid culture-medium?
How do you inoculate potato cultures?
In how many ways may gelatin tubes be inoculated?
What is meant by a stab-culture? By a slant culture?
How are plate cultures made?
Describe the method of making plate cultures according to Koch. How are agar plate cultures made?
How are colonies on plates counted?
Describe the method of making cultures in Petri dishes?
How are Esmarch's culture-tubes made?
Give a good method for the cultivation of anaërobic bacteria. What is an incubator?
What is a thermo-regulator?

CHAPTER V.

STERILIZATION, DISINFECTION, AND ANTISEPSIS.

Definitions.—The freeing of substances from the live bacteria they may contain or that may have collected on their surfaces is called **sterilization.** This is accomplished either by means of heat or the use of chemicals.

Erroneously sometimes the term sterilization is used to indicate the destruction of bacteria by the application of heat, the term disinfection being used then for their destruction by chemical agents.

To **disinfect** a substance is to destroy in it or on it all the harmful or infectious bacteria, without necessarily killing all the living bacteria.

THE METHODS OF STERILIZATION.

I. Substances **chemically sterilized are unfit for bacterial culture,** except in very rare instances when the chemical agents are very volatile.

II. In **laboratory work,** therefore, where the aim is the cultivation of bacteria, **heat** is the **only method of sterilization** used. This is applied either in the form of **dry heat** or **moist heat (steam).**

1. All substances which may be **passed through the Bunsen flame** and heated **red-hot** are usually sterilized in this manner.
2. Other implements, such as **instruments** and **glassware,** which would be **injured by the direct flame,** but **withstand considerable heat,** are sterilized by dry heat in an oven at a temperature of 160° to 180° C. for an hour.
3. For **culture-media,** one resorts to **sterilization by steam,** except in rare instances, when filtration under pressure through unglazed porcelain is considered sufficient.

Experience has taught that steam at a temperature of 100° C. will kill all known bacteria and their spores within an hour, and Pasteur has demonstrated that steam under a pressure of two or three atmospheres, at about 130° C., will destroy all known bacteria and their spores within fifteen or twenty minutes. *The sterilization of culture-media, then, is usually done by the means of steam, with or without pressure.*

4. In some instances, when exposure to steam for one hour would be prejudicial to the medium, what is known as **discontinuous** or **fractional sterilization** is resorted to. The medium is steamed during three consecutive days for twenty minutes each time; during the interval it is kept in favorable

FIG. 38.

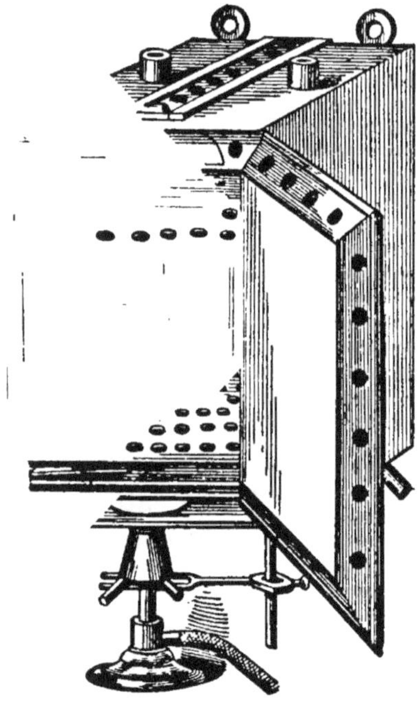

Laboratory hot-air sterilizer.

FIG. 39.

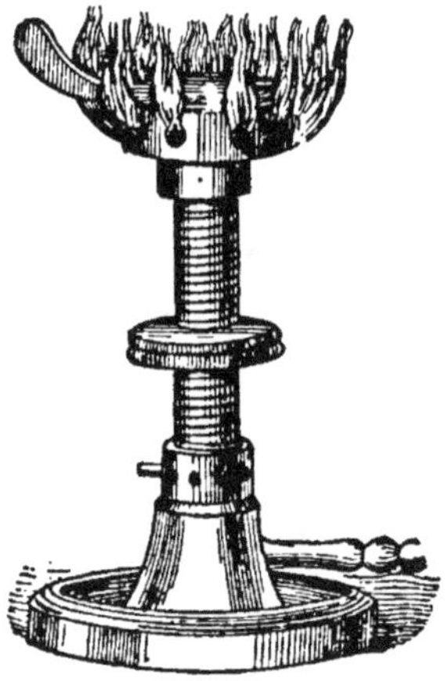

Rose-burner.

conditions for the development of bacteria. In this manner the first heat destroys all the fully formed bacteria that may exist. The favorable temperature in the interval between the first and second heatings allows all the spores contained in the medium which may not have been destroyed in the first heating to develop into fully formed germs, which are destroyed by the second application of steam on the ensuing day. The application of heat on the third day is to make sure of the destruction of all spores which may have resisted the two previous applications. It has been demonstrated that this sterilization is very effective and complete, and substances which have undergone it may be kept indefinitely **bacteria-free** thereafter.

5. **Another method of fractional sterilization** is occasionally used for certain media which cannot withstand the temperature of boiling water without deteriorating. It consists in

FIG. 40.

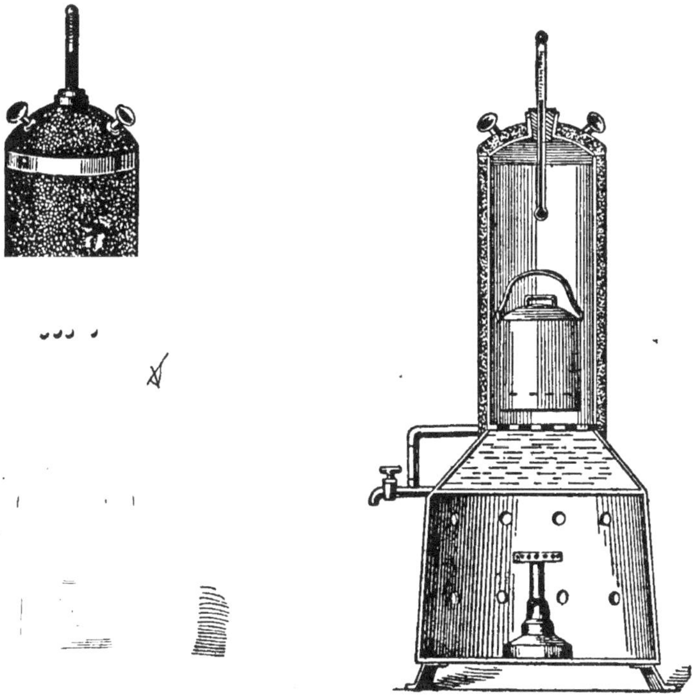

Steam sterilizer, pattern of Koch. (Abbott.)

submitting the medium to a temperature of 68° to 70° C. for from two to three hours during seven consecutive days. This method is necessarily very imperfect, and though successful in those cases in which no spores have to be destroyed and where none of the bacteria contained in the medium are of the pyrogenic variety, it cannot but have a very limited application, and media so sterilized should not be used for culture purposes, except after they have been submitted for several days to the temperature of the human body in the thermostat and remained sterile during this **control-test.**

6. For **generating dry heat** for the sterilization of **glass-ware, implements,** and **instruments** used in making cultures, the **hot-air oven and rose-burner** are most usually employed, and a temperature usually of 180° C. maintained in the oven for one and one-half hours (Figs. 38 and 39).

FIG. 41.

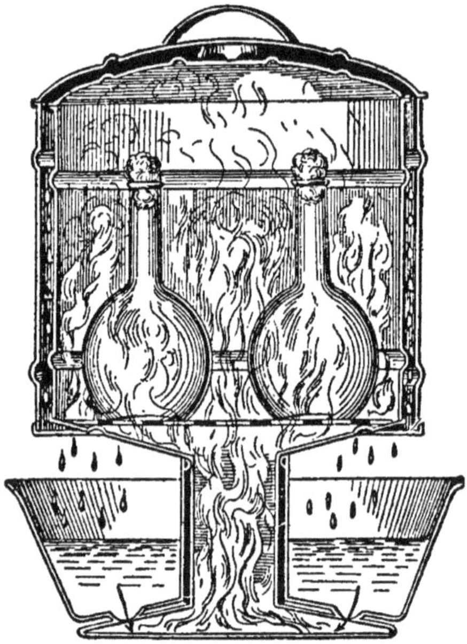

Arnold steam sterilizer. (Abbott.)

The oven **consists of** a double-walled metallic box, with a double-walled front door, with a copper bottom, the sides and door encased in asbestos boards. The heat is applied by means of a rose gas-burner (Fig. 39) to the bottom of the box. The objects to be sterilized are put upon perforated metallic shelves in the box. In the top of the apparatus are two perforated openings for the insertion of the thermometers. In this portion the oven is also provided with a perforated sliding window to allow escape of the overheated air.

7. For **applying moist heat**, bacteriologists commonly use *a*. **Koch's apparatus** (Fig. 40). *b*. **Arnold's apparatus** (Fig. 41).

8. For the **application of steam under pressure** preference is felt for the **autoclave of Chamberlain or of Wiesnegg** (Fig. 42).

9. For **discontinuous fractional sterilization at a low tem-**

FIG. 42.

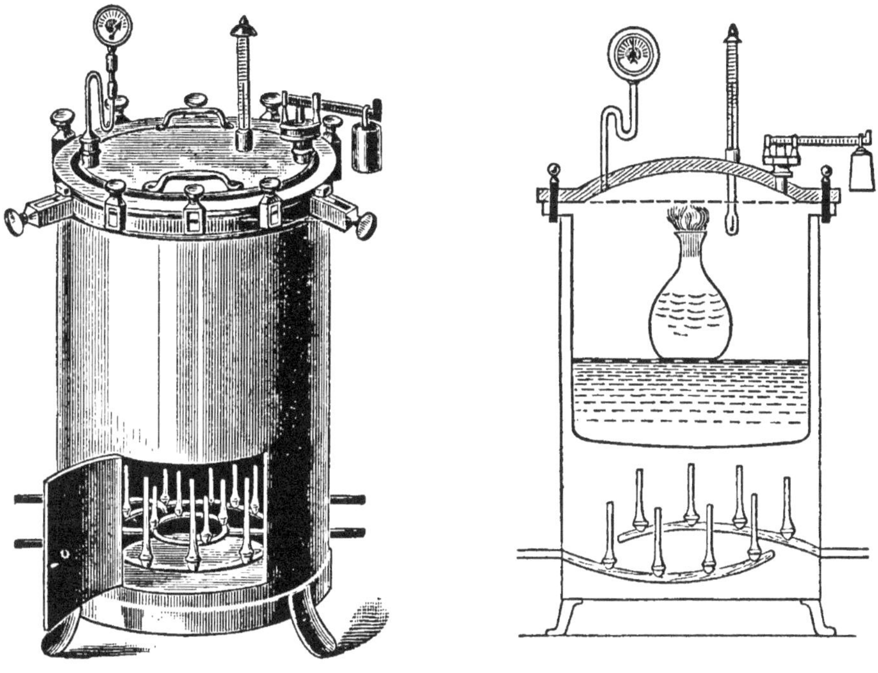

A *B*

Autoclave, pattern of Wiesnegg: *A*, external appearance; *B*, section. (Abbott.)

perature the apparatus in more general use is the **blood-serum sterilizer of Koch** (Fig. 43).

10. **Filtration under pressure through unglazed porcelain**, the pores of which are too small to allow bacteria to go through, will render certain liquid substances sterile or bacteria-free. This method is **made use of** in the case of certain pathogenic bacteria which secrete soluble poisons which we desire to separate from the bacteria themselves. The **Chamberlain**

filter of unglazed Sevre porcelain is the only one to be recommended for this purpose.

FIG. 43.

Chamber for sterilizing and solidifying blood-serum. (Koch.)

THE METHODS OF DISINFECTION.

I. **Disinfection** or **destruction of infectious bacteria** may with certainty be accomplished by **heat,** and indeed in the laboratory when the total destruction of the bacteria is desired with the material containing them **heat** is the most effective measure.

In other cases, however, when the **destruction of the bacteria** themselves and the **preservation of the contaminated substance** are desired, recourse must be had to such measures as will destroy the bacteria alone.

Substances which are able to destroy bacteria or their spores are known as **germicides** or **disinfectants,** and those substances which retard bacterial growth are called **antiseptics.**

II. In the **use of chemicals for disinfecting,** one should always bear in mind that their **mode of action** is not a catalytic one, but that they owe their virtue to the power of forming definite chemical compounds with the bacteria cells, which are thus rendered innocuous. They must, therefore, come into direct contact with the bacteria themselves, and in the combination so formed they and the bacteria change their chemical properties.

In the **choice of chemical disinfectants**, one must be guided by the species of bacteria to be destroyed, by the number of these bacteria, by the nature of the media containing the germs, by the substances to be disinfected, and by the quantity of material to be disinfected. All chemicals so used must be of a definite strength, and must be made to act for a specified time, the quantity and strength of the disinfectant and the time varying with the nature of the chemical and the species of bacteria to be destroyed.

To **test the germicidal power of substances**, the following is a convenient method: To young bouillon cultures of the bacteria to be acted upon sufficient of the chemical to be tested is added to make the proper dilution, and at given intervals of time a few droplets of this mixture are inoculated on sterile agar and gelatin tubes and the result carefully noted—for instance, supposing it is intended to test the germicidal power of carbolic acid toward some pus organism. To 9.90 c.c. of a bouillon culture of a pus germ in a test-tube 0.10 c.c. of carbolic acid is added, making the mixture a 1 per cent. carbolic acid dilution. The tube is well shaken, and at the end of one minute a few droplets of the mixture are taken on a sterile platinum needle and inoculated on a fresh tube of gelatin or agar, another fresh agar tube is inoculated with the mixture in the same manner after two minutes, another again after five minutes, and a fourth in fifteen minutes, a fifth in a half hour, a sixth in an hour, and a seventh in two hours. The growth in the inoculated tubes would indicate the action of 1 per cent. carbolic acid upon the given pus germ in the specified time. The same process is repeated, using a 2 per cent. dilution of the carbolic acid, and next a 3 per cent., a 4 per cent., and a 5 per cent. dilution. Higher than 5 per cent. solutions of carbolic acid are not possible with any but water too hot for this work.

In other substances a 10 per cent. dilution would be the last step of the test. Thus are obtained results which are fixed and definite, stating positively the strength of disinfection used and the time of its application.

Cautions.—In conducting these experiments one must remember always that the growth of bacteria on the solid tubes may be considerably retarded by the action of the disinfectants, and one must not accept the result as conclusive unless those cultures have been kept under observation for a considerable length of time. *Again it is proper, whenever practicable, to conduct the experiments at the temperature of the human body, 37° C., as experience has demonstrated that at this and higher temperature the disinfectant power of chemicals is increased.*

THE METHODS OF ANTISEPSIS.

Substances that retard the growth of bacteria without, however, destroying them are called **antiseptics.** It is clear that all disinfectants when used in a more diluted form, or when allowed to act for a shorter space of time than is required for them to show their germicidal power, act as antiseptics.

I. The Common Disinfectants.

Carbolic acid, strength 3 to 5 per cent., efficient in one hour.

Bichloride of mercury, solution 1 : 1000 or 1 : 500, acts from within a few minutes to a half-hour.

Chlorinated lime, containing free chlorine, is an efficient germicide in an hour's time in the strength of from 5 to 10 per cent.

Boiling water, to which 2 or 3 per cent. sodium carbonate is added, is an efficient germicide in an hour.

Sulphur dioxide gas, when used dry, has little or no disinfectant power, and bacteria have been able to withstand an atmosphere containing from 10 to 12 per cent. of this gas for several hours. In the presence of moisture, however, it forms sulphurous acid, and is then an efficient germicide in as low a percentage as 4 or 5 per cent.

Formalin, in 2 to 5 per cent. strength, or as **formaldehyde gas,** is a powerful germicide.

A number of other substances have been recommended, and have been used as germicides, but the above are of more general and practical value.

II. **Enumeration of the common antiseptics** would be too lengthy to be stated in a book of this kind.

In conclusion, one should bear in mind that **chemical agents** must act directly on the bacteria cells themselves—that is, they **must penetrate**; and that they are the more efficient the more quickly they form chemical compounds with those cells—or, as usually expressed, the more penetrating power they possess—and anything that interferes with this chemical combination interferes with the action of the disinfectant.

QUESTIONS.

What is meant by sterilization? By disinfection?

At what temperature and how long does it take dry heat to sterilize?

How long does it take live steam to sterilize?

How long does it take steam under pressure to sterilize?

How are implements in the bacteriological laboratory sterilized?

How are culture-media sterilized?

What is discontinuous or fractional sterilization by steam, and how is it accomplished?

How is sterilization at a low temperature effected? When is it used? What are its disadvantages?

What forms of apparatus are generally used to generate steam for sterilization?

What are the only filters which can remove bacteria from liquid media?

What are germicides or disinfectants?

What are antiseptics?

How would you test the value of a germicide?

What chemicals are generally used as disinfectants?

State the value of carbolic acid as a disinfectant; of bichloride of mercury; of the chlorinated lime; of sodium carbonate; of sulphur dioxide, and of formaldehyde.

CHAPTER VI.

THE INOCULATION OF ANIMALS AND THEIR STUDY.

THE INOCULATION OF ANIMALS.

Its **purposes** are to differentiate between bacteria. In order to study their virulence it is often necessary to test their action on animals.

In the laboratory the **smaller animals**, such as mice, rats, guinea-pigs, and rabbits, are chiefly used.

Technic.—The inoculation is made **in a number of ways**, depending on the species of the bacteria, the nature of its toxin, and the rapidity of action desired.

The Various Methods of Inoculation of Animals.

1. Sometimes, though rarely, the inoculation is made by **rubbing a solid or liquid culture over the abraded epidermis**, very much in the same manner as vaccine is introduced into the human subject.

2. **Subcutaneous inoculation**—that is, into the connective tissue under the skin—is an important method. For this purpose the hair is shaved from part of the back or abdomen, the skin well washed and disinfected as well as it may be, with a 5 per cent. carbolic acid solution. Then the skin is seized with a pair of sterilized forceps, and with a sterilized scalpel a small nick is made into it, after which a small sterilized pair of scissors is introduced in the areolar tissue and a **pocket** made for some little distance into this tissue. Into this pocket the inoculating material or bacterial culture (especially when a **solid** culture has been employed) is introduced, by means of a sterilized forceps or a platinum loop, *care being taken to avoid touching the edges of the wound with the instrument.*

If a **liquid culture** is being used, particularly in appreciable quantity, it may be introduced subcutaneously by means of a hypodermatic syringe and needle well sterilized beforehand.

Guinea-pigs and rabbits are usually inoculated in the abdominal wall; rats or mice in the loose tissue at the root of the tail.

Animal Holders.—Various instruments have been devised

FIG. 44.

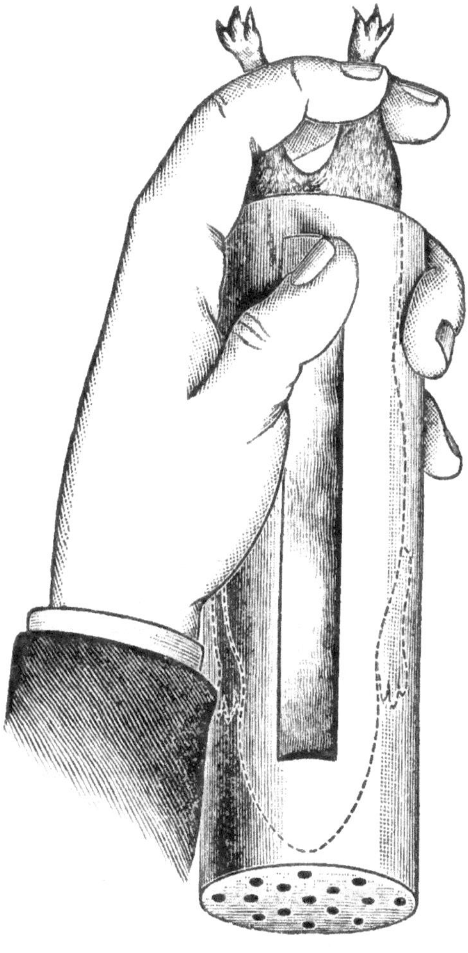

The Voges holder for guinea-pigs. (Abbott.)

for keeping animals quiet during this operation, the most useful of which are: **Voges' guinea-pig-holder** (Fig. 44); **Kitasato's mouse-holders** (Fig. 45); and the **basket mouse-holder** (Fig. 46).

3. **Intravenous injection** or **inoculation into the circulation**

consists in injecting directly into the veins of the animal in the direction of the circulation, the material to be inoculated. Necessarily the material used **must** be a **liquid,** and the injection must be done slowly and with precaution. Intravenous injection is used especially in rabbits. The **most convenient point of injection** is into the vein of the ear known as the **posterior auricular vein,** which is easily penetrated from the dorsal surface of the ear, where it lies superficial and

FIG. 45.

Kitasato's mouse-holder. (Abbott.)

FIG. 46.

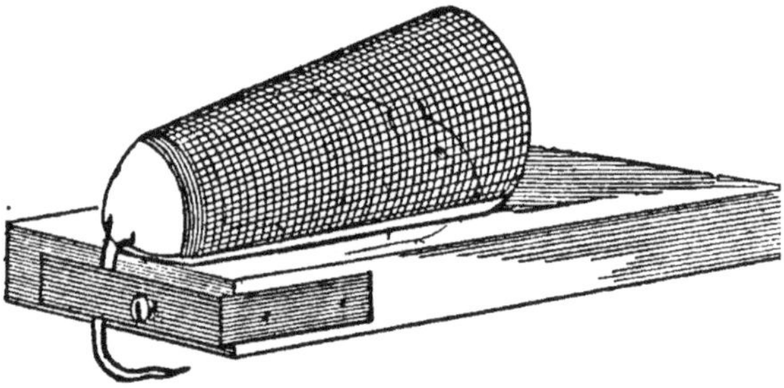

Mouse-holder, with mouse in proper position. (Abbott.)

imbedded firmly in the areolar tissue. For the purpose of making these injections an ordinary hypodermatic syringe with the needle used for morphine injections in man is employed. All that is required is that both syringe and needle be sterilized. The mode of procedure is as follows:

The rabbit is firmly held by an assistant. The ear chosen is taken between the thumb and forefinger of the left hand and after washing and sterilizing the skin as thoroughly as possible, the vein on the posterior edge of the ear is sought for. If it is invisible, pressure at the root of the ear will make it prominent.

From the dorsal surface the hypodermatic needle is inserted at its distal extremity and the material slowly injected. Care should be taken to have the needle penetrate the vein, and the first few drops of injected liquid will show whether it does so or not; for if the needle is outside the vein a bulla will immediately be found at the site of injection. A little practice renders this method very easy.

4. **Inoculation into the lymphatics** is done best with a hypodermatic syringe and the injection is made into the testicles.

5. **Intraperitoneal inoculation** requires much care and the same antiseptic precautions as when opening the peritoneum for a laparotomy. The skin, cleanly shaven and disinfected as thoroughly as possible, is opened in the linea alba midway between the sternum and pubis, through an incision, from an inch and a half to two inches long and penetrating the fascia. The edges of the wound being held apart, the connective tissue and muscles are separated with a pair of sterilized, blunt-pointed scissors. If a **liquid inoculating material** is used, it may now be introduced with a sterile hypodermatic needle into the peritoneal cavity, avoiding as much as possible the wounding of the intestines, which is not difficult. If the **material** employed is **solid**, the peritoneum is opened with scissors and the solid particle introduced into the cavity by means of a sterile needle or forceps. The wound is carefully sutured and closed by a layer of collodion.

6. **Intrapleural inoculation** is performed much more rarely on account of the danger of wounding the lungs, and when used the same precaution must be taken as for the intraperitoneal method.

7. **Inoculation into the anterior chamber of the eye** is performed occasionally to study in the living animal the changes produced locally by bacteria. With a sharp-pointed bistoury an incision is made in the cornea, at its sclerotic attachment near the inner canthus, and the material introduced and applied directly upon the iris, by a sterilized needle or by means of a small forceps.

THE OBSERVATION OF THE INOCULATED ANIMAL.

1. **After inoculation** animals should be observed carefully and all **changes in their condition** noted. Their **temperature** should be taken several times a day, their **body weight** recorded every day under the same conditions; their **behavior as to food** noticed; the **state of their fur** and any **sign of paralysis** or of **convulsions** carefully observed.

2. **After death**, the **autopsy** should be performed as soon as practicable. For that purpose the animal should be laid upon its back on a board, its four legs stretched widely apart and attached to the sides of the board by strings, or nailed, and the nose should also be carefully nailed down. By means of a 5 per cent. carbolic acid solution the skin of the body from the chin to the pubis should be carefully sterilized and all hair shaved off. The place of inoculation is now to be carefully examined and described.

Examination of the Abdominal and Pelvic Contents.—After this an incision is made in the skin only, and that carefully dissected away from the subcutaneous tissue and hooked back so as to prevent its contaminating the underlying tissues. After this by means of a metallic spatula, heated to redness, the muscular tissue is singed all along the line of the next incision, along the linea alba from the pubis to the sternum, along the arches of the rib and obliquely from the sterno-clavicular junctions to the tip of the last two ribs. With a pair of sterilized blunt-pointed scissors the **peritoneal cavity is opened.** All changes within it are carefully noted, cultures made from all exudates, or inflammatory products apparent, bouillon, agar, and blood-serum tubes being used for that purpose, and cover-glasses being also prepared for the microscope. Then, by means of the same heated spatula, the surfaces of the different organs are thoroughly singed, and with a spear-head, thick sterilized platinum wire, the organ is penetrated and cultures made from the small pieces of organs or blood adhering to the wire; bouillon, agar, and blood-serum being used, and cover-glasses being also prepared.

From all cultures so obtained plate cultures should be made, and the several bacteria therein isolated, and pure cultures made.

After complete examination of the abdominal and pelvic organs, by means of a thick pair of scissors the ribs are cut off along the singed lines, the sternum turned up, and **examination and cultures of the thoracic organs** made in the same way as for the abdominal organs.

3. **Arter the complete autopsy** the animal should be incinerated, and if this is not practicable, it should be kept bathed at least for two hours in a 5 per cent. carbolic acid solution, and finally boxed in quicklime before burial.

Cultures from the human body at autopsies should be made as described for lower animals.

4. **Cultures from secretions of living animals and man** should be made immediately upon their passage and must be always collected in sterilized vessels. The examinations and the cultures should be prepared forthwith, using agar, bouillon, and serum as media.

The Roux-Nocard Method of Culture and Observation.

History.—Recently observations made by Roux and Nocard for the growth of microörganisms in culture in the live animal have shown that a number of minute bacteria are found associated with certain diseases, notably the pleuropneumonia of cattle. These microörganisms require a much higher power of the microscope than that generally in use to bring them into view, a magnification of 2000 at least being necessary.

Technic.—Small collodion flasks are made thoroughly sterile, filled with blood from the suspected animal, and then closed with sterile collodion. These tubes or flasks are afterward introduced into the abdominal cavity of live rabbits and guinea-pigs, and allowed to remain for a few days, after which they are taken out and examined, when the small motile microörganisms as mentioned above will be discovered.

Importance.—This method of observation and cultivation in the live animal body seems to open a large field for the future investigation of such diseases as scarlet fever, measles, smallpox, rabies, etc., which, though unquestionably of microbic origin, have so far failed to reveal any specific germ for their causation.

QUESTIONS.

Why are animals inoculated?

What different methods are used for animal inoculation in the laboratory?

Describe the subcutaneous method. The intravenous method. The intra-lymphatic method. The intraperitoneal method.

What instruments are used to inoculate liquid cultures into the veins of animals?

What should be observed in inoculated animals?

How should an autopsy be made in the case of an animal dead after inoculation?

What precautions are necessary in making cultures from tissues and organs in dead animals to prevent contamination from outside?

How should secretions of animals and men be collected for bacterial examination?

What form of culture have Roux and Nocard proposed for cultivation of bacteria?

CHAPTER VII.

INFECTION AND IMMUNITY.

INFECTION.

BACTERIA which **produce diseases in animals** and **man** are known as the **pathogenic bacteria,** and the **process** by which disease is produced is called **infection.**

The **mode of communication** of these infections to man or to animals is not fully demonstrated. The following explanations are the more plausible.

The Theories of Infection.

1. The **rapid multiplication of bacteria in the blood and organs** of infected animals is supposed to interfere with their bodily functions, and so cause disease and death. This is the so-called **mechanical theory of infection,** and finds support in such diseases as anthrax, when in fatal cases every capillary

and organ of the animal is teeming with microörganisms, and in so-called septicæmic diseases where the microörganisms may be found in greater or lesser number in the blood and organs.

II. The **bacteria secrete or contain in their cell-bodies poisonous substances (toxins)** which act deleteriously on the animal economy through its own molecules. This, the **chemical theory**, is the accepted one of to-day, and finds its ready explanation in nearly all infectious diseases, especially in those which, like diphtheria and tetanus, may be superinduced by inoculations of cultures from which the bacteria have been eliminated by filtration. The so-called **toxæmic diseases** are so produced.

The Avenues and Factors of Infection.

A. Infection of the animal body is effected by **one of three ways**:

I. Through the **respiratory tract.**

II. Through the **digestive tract.**

III. Through the **wounded** or **unwounded surface of the skin** or **mucous membrane.**

B. **Conditions and Factors.**—These are various and play an important part in infection. Some of them have reference (1) to the **infecting material,** or chiefly (2) to the **animal** experimented upon. To the first class belong the species of bacteria, the quantity of infected material introduced, the cultural conditions of the bacteria, the presence or absence of the so-called mixed infection in which more than one species is taking part, the method of its introduction, and, in some cases, the time elapsed since the infection occurred. The conditions which depend upon the animal are the following: the amount of natural resistance to the bacterial poison, the condition of health of the animal.

It must be remembered that some species of bacteria are much more injurious than others either on account of the rapidity with which they are able to develop in the human or animal economy, or on account of the large quantity of toxins which they generate, or on account of the highly poisonous property of these toxins.

1. The **quantity of bacteria** used plays an important part because there is a more or less marked natural resistance in the animal body to the action of bacteria or their poisons. When these are introduced in small quantity only, they fail to produce any effect, and it requires a certain definite amount of bacteria to produce disease in the animal body. This amount varies with the species of the bacteria.

2. The **condition of the bacterial culture** when introduced into the animal body is an important factor in the subsequent course of the infection, for bacteria under different conditions secrete toxins which are more or less injurious, and the same bacteria grown under the same conditions are able at different times to produce toxins of more or less virulence. When the condition of growth or the environment of the bacteria varies, their cultural aspects and the amount of toxins they are able to produce vary also. So much so is this the case that bacteria are grown under peculiarly disadvantageous surroundings—high temperature, or the addition of a small proportion of antiseptics to their cultural fluid so as to produce bacteria of less virulence—in other words, to **attenuate** them.

Methods of Attenuation.—Bacteria from young liquid cultures are known to be more virulent than those from older cultures. Again, cultures are made through the body of resisting animals so as to diminish the virulence of the cultures. Or, again, the cultures are passed through artificial media for a number of generations to diminish their virulence. The converse of this happens also, and bacteria grown or passed through the bodies of susceptible animals acquire more and more virulence.

3. The **method of introduction of the bacteria** contributes considerably to the degree of infection from the fact that nearly all bacteria have certain affinities for different tissues of the body where they exert their most baneful influence, and the nearer akin to those tissues is the place of the introduction in the body the more rapidly and energetically is the

bacterial influence felt. Again, the different secretions of the body have more or less germicidal effect, so that bacteria, as a rule, are more potent in their effect when introduced directly into the circulation.

4. The **association of bacteria among themselves** has occasionally the power of increasing the toxic effects of the inoculated germs, sometimes the two germs acting simultaneously on the animal body and producing what is known as "**double**," "**mixed**," or "**associated**" **infection.** At other times, some of the germs, though not pathogenic, are able to destroy the resistance of the body to the action of other toxic germs, as, for instance, the injection of tetanus bacillus with some ordinary saprophyte is capable of producing symptoms when the introduction of the tetanus germs alone would utterly fail.

Occasionally a **beneficial association of germs** may be observed, the presence of the secretion of some bacteria being prejudicial to the growth of other bacteria or neutralizing their toxins.

5. The **condition of the human or animal body as to perfect health**, as has already been remarked, offers more or less resistance to the bacterial poison. When, however, the general health is below par this resistance is diminished and the animal is much more susceptible to the action of the germs.

6. The **time elapsed since the infection** is often of great moment. In some cases germs will lurk in an organ for a long time, after which, through circumstances very little understood, they will suddenly and violently begin to cause symptoms and often death. Diseases of the appendix and gall-bladder in man are among the more familiar examples of this phenomenon.

IMMUNITY AND ITS VARIETIES.

Resistance to the action of pathogenic bacteria is called immunity, and is either **natural** or **acquired.**

I. **Natural immunity** is present in all such cases where, for instance, some species of animals can not be affected by certain bacteria or their toxins, which are injurious to other species, or, as occasionally happens, when some individuals in a susceptible species are refractive.

II. **Acquired immunity** is manifested when a susceptible animal is protected from the further noxious influences of bacteria either from the fact of having suffered an attack of the disease caused by the bacteria, or when it has been made artificially insusceptible.

Examples of Natural Immunity.—Rats can not be successfully inoculated with the anthrax bacillus, though other rodents are very susceptible. Again, pigeons are not susceptible but are immune to the anthrax bacillus. The explanation of this natural immunity is not easily given. It is supposed in some cases to be due to the mode of living of the immune animal, or to some condition of its secretions, or to some substances found in its blood and tissues which are able to destroy bacterial life or to neutralize their toxins. These substances are called **alexins.**

Examples of Acquired Immunity.—This may be due, as just mentioned, to a previous attack of disease, and when due to this it lasts in the majority of instances during the life of the animal. In other cases acquired immunity can be artificially induced in animals, and according to the methods used for its production is said to be active or passive.

1. **Active acquired immunity** is produced by the action of living germs or their toxins introduced into the animal.

2. **Passive acquired immunity** is obtained by a direct transference of an immunizing substance from an immune animal to a susceptible one. Active immunity takes some time to develop, but, as a rule, lasts longer than passive immunity, which is immediately established.

The Methods of Producing Immunity.

I. **Inoculation, or the introduction of small quantities of live bacteria,** so as to produce a mild attack of the disease. This method is dangerous from the fact that it is hard to ascertain how small a quantity of bacteria may be introduced without its being prejudicial to life, and from the danger of spreading the infection.

II. **Vaccination, or the introduction of attenuated bacteria,** which attenuation is obtained either by submitting the bacteria to a higher degree of heat during their cultivation or by adding a small proportion of an antiseptic to their culture-media, or by using bacteria which have grown for a long period of time in artificial media, or by using bacteria which have grown in the bodies of natural immunes.

III. **Intoxication,** or **the introduction of the toxins of the bacteria** in small broken but frequently repeated doses, or in cases where the toxic effect of bacteria is due to substances contained in the cell-body itself by the injection of the dead bacilli. This is the method used for the production of the diphtheria and tetanus antitoxins.

IV. **Antitoxins,** or **the introduction of bacterial products** of any one of the first three processes into other animals, these substances, known by the name of antitoxins, being able to confer immunity to susceptible animals.

V. By the **inoculation of an emulsion of tissues,** consisting in the introduction into the animal of the emulsion of certain tissues which are known to be the tissues susceptible to the action of the bacterial poison.

VI. By **introducing** into the animal **inert particles,** such as carmine, mixed with the bacteria.

Forced immunization of animals consists in introducing gradually and in increasing doses bacterial toxins in sufficient quantity to produce a reaction, but in quantity too small to produce deleterious effects. In this way it has been found that animals immunized produce substances in their tissue-fluids which when inoculated in susceptible animals serve to protect them against the deleterious action of those bacteria or their toxins.

The Antitoxic and Antimicrobic Blood-Serums.

The **blood-serum of animals** used for the purpose of protecting others is said to be **antitoxic,** when it has been obtained by the action of the toxins of the bacteria on the animal; and to be **antimicrobic**, when it has been obtained by means of the action of virulent or attenuated cultures on those animals.

Uses.—Antitoxic serum is employed chiefly in the toxic diseases, such as diphtheria, tetanus, etc., and **antimicrobic serum** is used particularly in the invasive diseases, such as plague, typhoid fever, cholera, etc.

Theories in Explanation.—A number have been suggested. Some believe that the antitoxin is a chemically changed toxin; others claim that it is a sort of enzyme produced by the toxin; others again state that it is the product of the cytic activity developed by the toxin; again others consider that it acts as a sort of combining ferment in the same manner as those ferments which favor coagulation of the fibrin in the blood.

The Theories of Immunity.

How these substances act so as to produce immunity in animals is a subject that has occupied investigators considerably in recent years.

I. **The abstraction theory (Pasteur's)** is to-day only of historical interest. It was believed to be due to the fact that the pabulum necessary for the life of the specific bacteria had been consumed, and that these bacteria could no longer live in the animal.

II. **The retention theory (Chauveau's)**, in which it was supposed that microörganisms left in the system certain substances which were antagonistic to their further growth, is still worthy to-day of some consideration.

III. The **theory of phagocytosis (Metchnikoff's)**, by which immunity was supposed to be due to the action of the white blood-corpuscles, which have the power of absorbing and destroying bacteria, is not tenable to-day in its original entirety. That the leucocytes play a certain part in the immunizing process cannot be denied, but the phagocytic property is more probably due to the fact that the animal is immune than the cause of the immunization.

Immunity is, in general terms, certainly produced by certain secretions formed in the animal's body, and secreted by it to protect itself from the attack of the invading bacteria, and distributed in all the tissues, but found especially in the serum of the blood.

IV. The **chain-theory (Ehrlich's)** claims that this immunizing substance is developed on account of the fact that the poisonous substances introduced by the microbes or the secretions of the microbes in the animal body combine with certain elements of the tissue and destroy them, subtracting them from other elements with which they were naturally in combination; this stimulates the natural resistance of the tissues and causes an increased production of the substances attacked by the bacteria in such a way that an overproduction results, and this makes the animal more resistant to the further introduction of the poison. This is certainly the most plausible explanation of immunity offered to this day.

A passing remark, however, may only be offered on this subject, and those who are interested must be directed to consult larger works, in which these views are explained at length.

QUESTIONS.

What is infection?

How are bacteria called which produce disease in animals?

How is the action of pathogenic bacteria on the animal body explained?

When is a disease said to be septicæmic? When is it toxæmic?

Name the three modes by which the animal body may be infected.

What conditions favor infection?

What conditions in the infecting material increase its power?

What conditions in the animal increase the rapidity of infection?

What part does the quantity of bacteria introduced in the inoculation play in the infection?

What is meant by attenuation?

What conditions of the cultures make the bacteria more virulent?

What is the effect of passing for a number of generations pathogenic bacteria through artificial media?

What part does the mode of introduction of the bacteria in the animal body play in infection?

What is meant by double infection?

What is immunity?

What is meant by natural immunity?

What is meant by acquired immunity?

Give some examples of natural immunity?

What produces acquired immunity in animals?

What are active and passive immunity?
What artificial methods are used to produce immunity?
What is meant by inoculation? Vaccination? Intoxication?
How does tissue suspension produce immunity?
What influence does the injection of inert particles have upon immunity?
What is meant by forced immunity?
What is meant by an antitoxic serum? By an antimicrobic serum?
What classes of disease are protected against by antitoxic serum? What by antimicrobic serum?
How is this anti-action explained?
What is the theory of abstraction?
What is meant by the retention theory?
What is the theory of Metchnikoff?
What is Ehrlich's chain-theory?

CHAPTER VIII.

THE PATHOGENIC BACTERIA.

THE PYOGENIC MICROCOCCI AND ALLIED BACILLI.

THE most commonly found **bacteria in pus** are **cocci (pyococci)**. A few are **bacilli**. The list includes:

1. The *Staphylococcus pyogenes aureus, albus*, and *citreus;* the *Staphylococcus cereus albus*, the *Staphylococcus cereus aureus* (**Passet**); the *Staphylococcus cereus flavus* (**Passet**).

2. The *Micrococcus pyogenes tenuis* (Rosenbach). The *Micrococcus tetragenus* is sometimes found associated with the foregoing two varieties in abscesses or in pus cavities, and are also able to produce abscesses at the place of injection in animals.

3. The *Streptococcus pyogenes* is found associated with the staphylococci in purulent accumulations, and is sometimes itself responsible for pus-production in the body.

4. The **gonococcus** is the cause of specific suppuration of the urethra and often elsewhere in the body.

5. The **pneumococcus** is often found in abscesses which occur in the course of the disease in pneumonic patients.

6, 7, and 8. The *Bacillus pyocyaneus, typhosus*, and *tuberculosis* are sometimes the cause of pus-production, as pure cultures of these organisms have been found in some cases of abscesses during the respective infections.

Nearly all pyogenic organisms are facultative anaërobics.

THE INDIVIDUAL FEATURES OF THE PYOGENIC BACTERIA.

I. Staphylococcus Pyogenes Aureus.

The *Staphylococcus pyogenes aureus*, by far the **most frequent** pus organism, **is found** *a.* **in health** on the surface of the skin, also of the mucous membranes in the digestive tube, and upper part of the respiratory tract, and *b.* **in pathological conditions** in pus irrespective of its localization, either alone or in association with the other pyogenic staphylococci, also

FIG. 47.

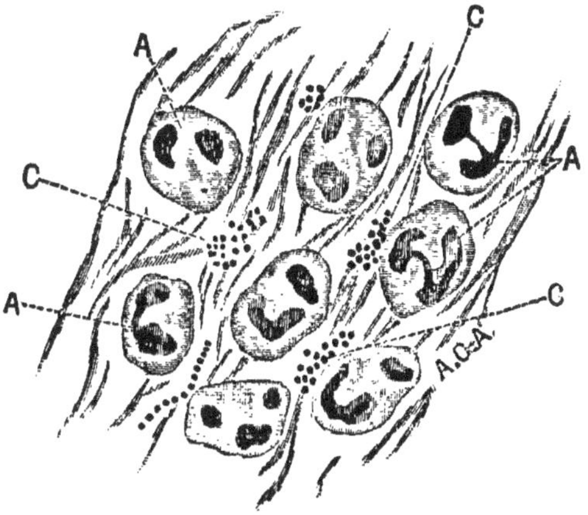

Preparation from pus, showing pus-cells, *A*, and staphylococci, *C*. (Abbott.)

in the blood in cases of general infection, and a number of cases of extensive suppurating lesions, abscesses, suppurating tumors, furuncles, etc.; and *c.* **outside of the human body** in the air, in dust, and occasionally in water.

Morphology.—The *Staphylococcus pyogenes aureus* is a small rounded cell, having a diameter of 0.9 to 1.2 mikrons, found either singly or in irregular groups or masses resembling a bunch of grapes, hence its name. Sometimes it is seen in pairs, as a diplococcus. Its appearance in pus as well as in culture-media is the same in general as is seen in Fig. 47.

Principal Biologic Characters.—The *Staphylococcus pyogenes aureus* is a **facultative anaërobic.** It clouds **bouillon** in twenty-four hours at 37° C., and shows from the second day a yellowish precipitate, which gradually increases in color and at the bottom of the tube appears of a golden yellow. It liquefies **gelatin.** Stab-cultures on this media at 20° C. on the second or third day have the appearance of a funnel, at the bottom of which is an orange-yellow deposit. At the end of three days the gelatin in the tube is completely liquefied. On gelatin plates colonies of a dark-yellowish color are observed with a centre of more or less intense orange color.

On **agar-agar** the colonies appear small, regularly spherical, and of an orange-yellow. Plates made from this medium have the same characteristics as on gelatin, being more or less pigmented yellow. It does not liquefy agar. The cultures on **blood-serum** have the same characteristics as on agar. The *Staphylococcus pyogenes aureus* stains with all the anilin dyes, and also by Gram's method.

Pathogenesis.—When inoculated into the **blood** of an animal, the *Staphylococcus aureus* rapidly causes a fatal septicæmia. Rabbits and guinea-pigs die, as a rule, in twenty-four to forty-eight hours after inoculation, and the organisms may be found generally disseminated in the blood-capillaries of the organs, and are also found in the blood taken from the heart. Inoculations into the **peritoneal cavity** cause a purulent peritonitis of a virulent character, generally ending in death of the animal. Injected **under the skin,** this organism produces localized abscesses.

II. Staphylococcus Pyogenes Albus.

The *Staphylococcus pyogenes albus,* like its companion the aureus, exists as a saprophyte: *a.* on the surface of the skin in man, and *b.* in association with the aureus in abscesses and superficial phlegmons.

Although clinicians are in the habit of considering it as an

achromogenic variety of the preceding, it is, however, somewhat **less pathogenic.** Its **morphological characters** are the same as those of the aureus, with the exception that it does not form pigment and its colonies are of a milk-white color.

III. Staphylococcus Citreus.

The *Staphylococcus pyogenes citreus* is of identical **morphology** with the two preceding varieties, with the exceptions that its **growth** is of a lemon-yellow color and that it liquefies gelatin more slowly. It is **found** in association with the *Staphylococcus aureus* and *albus* in pus of acute abscesses, especially in the liver.

IV. Streptococcus Pyogenes.

The *Streptococcus pyogenes* **is found**: *a.* in the lymphatics of the skin in patients suffering from erysipelas, *b.* in pus, *c.* in the false membranes in cases of diphtheria, *d.* in surgical and *e.* obstetrical complications of erysipelas, and *f.* as a frequent causative agent of puerperal septicæmia and of many surgically common infections (Fig. 48 and Plate I.).

FIG. 48.

Streptococcus pyogenes. (Abbott.)

Morphology.—The streptococcus is a micrococcus varying in size from 1 to 4 mikrons in diameter, spherical in shape and arranged as a chain of variable length. When grown in liquid media, this chain consists of from 30 to 40 elements, but in solid media a chain usually consists of from 7 to 10 cocci. In young cultures the diameters of all the cocci of the

PLATE I.

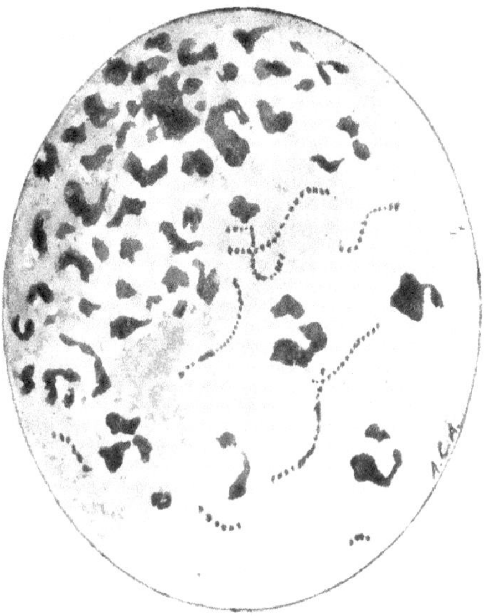

Streptococcus Pyogenes in Pus. (Abbott.)

chain are equal; in older cultures they vary very much even in the same chain.

Biologic Characters.—The streptococcus is **aërobic** and **facultative anaërobic.** At 37° C. it clouds **bouillon** in twenty-four hours, and this becomes again clear at the end of three or four days, when small spherical bodies may be seen at the bottom of the tube. The bouillon becomes acid. On **gelatin** it forms small spherical opaque colonies about the size of a pin-head, which cease to increase after the third or fourth day. It does not liquefy gelatin. On **agar-agar** also it forms spherical colonies of the size of a pin-head, semitransparent and of a grayish-white appearance, shaped somewhat like a bead. It does not develop **on potato.** *The streptococcus does not live longer than three weeks in cultures.* It **stains** by the Gram method, and also by the other anilin dyes.

Pathogenesis.—**Intravenous** inoculations in animals produce variable effects. The germ usually kills the animal, causing a rapid general septicæmia; at other times the animal reacts only slightly. **Subcutaneously** it causes erysipelas and the formation of abscesses. *All laboratory animals are susceptible to infection by means of the streptococcus pyogenes.*

V. The Micrococcus Cereus Albus.

VI. The Micrococcus Cereus Flavus.

These **were found** in pus by **Passet** associated with other organisms. Their **pathogenesis** has not been fully established. They **differ** from the other groups of cocci just described by the shiny, waxy appearance of their growth.

VII. The Micrococcus Pyogenes Tenuis.

This **was found** in pus by **Rosenbach,** is very **irregular** in **size** and somewhat larger than the *Staphylococcus albus.* On **agar-agar** its **biology** presents a thin opaque streak along the line of inoculation, resembling a thin layer of varnish. Its **pathogenic properties** have never been fully determined.

VIII. Micrococcus Tetragenus.

The *Micrococcus tetragenus* was **obtained by Koch** *a.* from cavities of tuberculous lungs, *b.* in the sputum of phthisical patients in the last stages of the disease, *c.* in the pus of buccal and *d.* ocular abscesses. It **has been found by Morinier** *e.* in the normal saliva and *f.* even in the saliva of newborn babes.

Morphology.—A micrococcus with a diameter of about 1 mikron, formed in groups of 8 (tetrads) and enveloped by a transparent gelatinous substance.

Principal Biologic Properties.—It is a **facultative anaërobic.** On **agar** it forms thick granular spherical colonies of a white or grayish color. It does not liquefy **gelatin.** It **stains** with all the anilin dyes and readily by Gram's method.

Pathogenesis.—When inoculated into guinea-pigs **subcutaneously,** the animals die rapidly and abscesses are formed at the point of inoculation. The micrococcus at the autopsy may be found in all the organs and in the blood taken from the heart.

GONORRHŒA.

IX. Micrococcus Gonorrhœæ (Gonococcus).

Discovered by Neisser in 1879, the gonococcus **causes** the specific suppuration of gonorrhœa.

Pathogenesis.—This micrococcus, or **diplococcus,** as it is generally called, has a special affinity for the urethral mucous membrane, finding lodgement in the epithelial cells lining this canal. It sometimes causes inflammation with or without suppuration in other parts of the human body, such as the conjunctiva, appendages of the uterus, in the peritoneum and articulations. Cutaneous and muscular abscesses have occasionally been found to be caused by the gonococcus.

Morphology.—These micrococci are usually found **united in pairs** presenting the appearance of grains of coffee, the two opposing sides being generally flattened or concave. In stained preparations the flattened surfaces are separated by **an** unstained interspace. The gonococci **are found** free in the pus, but more often as small masses in the pus or epithelial cells. This serves partly to distinguish them from other pus cocci (Fig. 49).

Principal Biologic Characters.—It is **aerobic**, but is very difficult to cultivate outside the human body. A number of investigators have succeeded in cultivating it on **human blood-serum** obtained from the placenta of a recently delivered woman; others have been successful with **ascitic fluid** and with the **fluid of hydrocele.** The cultures grow at a temperature of between 30° and 35° C. Finger has succeeded in cultivating it in **sterile acid urine with 0.5 per cent. of peptone.**

FIG. 49.

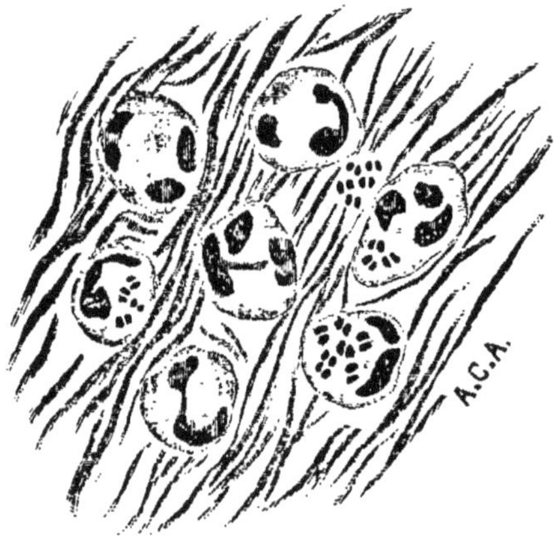

Pus of gonorrhœa, showing diplococci in the bodies of the pus-cells. (Abbott.)

The gonococcus will not grow on gelatin, agar-agar, potato, or in bouillon.

It **stains** with the basic anilin dyes, especially with gentian-violet. It does **not stain** by the Gram method. This is a valuable point to differentiate it from the pus cocci, which all stain by the Gram method.

Pathogenesis.—Toure succeeded in causing urethritis **in dogs** by injecting **into their urethras** cultures in acid media. Finger and Golm have caused acute urethritis, which rapidly disappeared, **by intra-articular injections** of cultures into dogs and rabbits. Pus containing the gonococci when **inoculated into**

man have reproduced the disease in many instances. Pus cultures of the gonococci have also given positive results in many cases: Wertheim, 5 times in 5 cases; Bockardt, 6 times in 10 cases; Finger, 3 times in 14 cases. **Subcutaneous injections** of the culture produce considerable tumefaction and redness at the point of inoculation, but no abscess-formation.

X. Bacillus Pyocyaneus.

The *Bacillus pyocyaneus* **is found** frequently in suppurating wounds, especially in burns. It colors the pus green and the dressings a bluish-green, without showing any color-influence on the local condition of the wound.

Pathogenesis.—It exists in pus associated with other micro-organisms, and is considered an inoffensive saprophyte in most cases. It may, however, under certain conditions become pathogenic.

Morphology.—It is a delicate rod with rounded or pointed ends.

Biologic Characters.—It is aërobic and grows readily on all artificial media and imparts to them a bright-green color. It liquefies gelatin and stains readily with all anilin dyes.

XI. Bacillus Pyogenes Fœtidus.

This organism was first **obtained by Passet** from suppurating surfaces in the vicinity of the lower bowel.

Morphology.—It is a short bacillus with rounded ends, usually found in pairs or in short chains.

Biology.—It is an **aërobic**, motile, and grows **on all media. Stains** with all the anilin dyes. The cultures are noted on account of the disagreeable putrefactive odor which they emit. It derives its name from this feature.

XII. Pneumococcus or Pneumobacillus.

Friedlaender discovered this organism. It is sometimes **found**: *a.* in pus associated with other organisms and *b.* in cases of pneumonia as the sole factor of the disease and its secondary abscesses. The pus produced by it is thick, and creamy white in color.

Pathogenesis.—It frequently causes suppuration in the serous membranes—pleura, peritoneum, pericardium, and lungs. It has also on some occasions caused suppuration in the viscera and in the subcutaneous and deep cellular tissue.

XIII. Bacillus Coli Communis.

XIV. Bacillus Typhosus.

XV. Bacillus Tuberculosis.

These three organisms are **sometimes found** associated with pus-formation, and have been thought to be occasionally the chief suppurative agents. The discussion of this subject, however, will be properly taken up under the head of the description of these bacilli.

QUESTIONS.

What are the pyococci?

Describe the *Staphylococcus pyogenes aureus*. How does it act on bouillon, on gelatin, on agar?

Where is this organism found in the human body? Where outside of the human body?

What is the effect on animals of intravenous injections of this organism? What of subcutaneous inoculation?

In what respect does the *Staphylococcus pyogenes albus* differ from the aureus? The *Staphylococcus pyogenes citreus?*

Describe the streptococcus pyogenes. Where is it found? Of how many elements are its chains formed? What is the effect of intravenous, intraperitoneal, and subcutaneous inoculations?

Where were the *Micrococcus cereus albus* and *flavus* found, and by whom?

What are the characteristics of the *Micrococcus tetragenus?*

What is the gonococcus? Where is it found? How is it recognized under the microscope?

What media are best suited for its growth? How is it differentiated from other pus cocci?

What other bacteria cause suppuration or are found in pure cultures in abscesses.

CHAPTER IX.

THE OTHER PATHOGENIC MICROCOCCI AND ALLIED BACILLI—MICROCOCCUS PNEUMONIÆ, EPIDEMIC CEREBROSPINAL MENINGITIS, AND MALTA FEVER.

PNEUMONIA.

I. Micrococcus Pneumoniæ Crouposæ (Diplococcus Pneumoniæ; Micrococcus Pasteuri; Micrococcus of Sputum Septicæmia).

History.—The *Micrococcus pneumoniæ crouposæ* was **discovered** in September, 1880, by **Sternberg,** in the blood of rabbits which he had inoculated subcutaneously with his own saliva; also by **Pasteur,** in December, 1880, in the saliva of a child who had died of pneumonia in a Paris hospital. This was **confirmed** and **studied** by **Fraenkel, Weichselbaum,** and others.

It **is found:** *a.* in the saliva of about 50 per cent. of healthy individuals, *b.* in the rusty sputum of pneumonic patients and in the fibrinous exudation of 75 per cent. of the cases of pneumonia, *c.* in a large number of cases of meningitis complicating pneumonia or associated with pneumonia, *d.* **occasionally** where no pneumonia exists, *e.* also in abscesses.

Morphology.—*Micrococcus pneumoniæ* is a small oval coccus appearing alone or united in pairs, occasionally forming chains with four or five elements resembling streptococci. In the animal body it is generally oval and double, as a **diplococcus, surrounded by a capsule** (Fig. 50).

In **solid media** it grows as a micrococcus, a diplococcus, or as a chain like the streptococcus with scarcely more than four or five elements. In **liquid media** the cells are more nearly round, and the chains contain sometimes as many as eight or ten elements (Fig. 51).

It **stains** by the anilin dyes, and also by Gram's method.

Biologic Characters.—The *Micrococcus pneumoniæ* is **aërobic** and **facultative anaërobic.** Like most cocci it is non-motile,

FIG. 50.

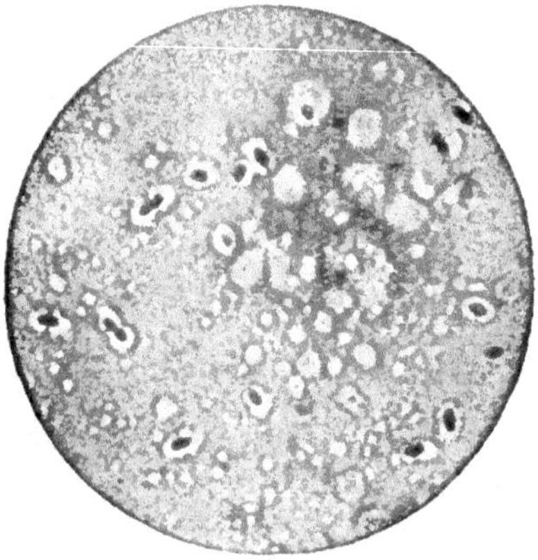

Diplococcus of pneumonia from blood, with surrounding capsule. (Park.)

and therefore has no flagella. It grows on all culture-media, very little at a temperature below 24° C., best at a temperature of 37° C. At a temperature above 42° C. all growth

FIG. 51.

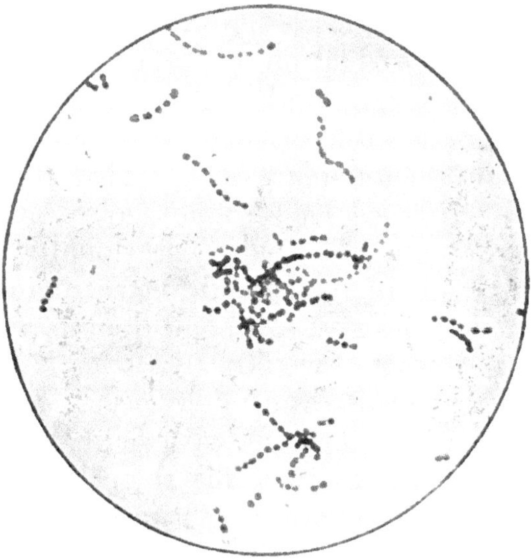

Pneumococcus from bouillon culture, resembling streptococcus. (Park.)

ceases. It is killed in a few minutes by exposure to a temperature of 52° C. If grown at 42° C. for twenty-four hours, its culture becomes very much attenuated, practically losing its virulence.

In **bouillon** it grows rapidly, and in twenty-four hours causes a distinct cloudiness of the medium. At the end of forty-eight hours its growth ceases, and in four or five days the bouillon becomes clear again, the bacillary growth being deposited at the bottom of the tube. In **15 per cent. gelatin** at 24° C. its growth is slow. The gelatin is not liquefied. On **blood-serum** at the temperature of 37° C. it grows as clear, almost transparent spots. Its growth **on agar** is very much like that on blood-serum. It does not grow on **potato.** It causes coagulation of **milk.**

Immunization.—The inoculation of animals with **attenuated cultures** grown at 42° C. for twenty-four hours seems to protect the animal from the after-infection of virulent cultures. An infusion made of the tissues of immunized animals seems to have a protective influence when injected simultaneously or shortly before virulent cultures in susceptible animals.

Pathogenesis.—Mice and rabbits are very susceptible to the action of the *Micrococcus pneumoniæ*, guinea-pigs much less so. When **injected subcutaneously** into mice and rabbits, it produces a general septicæmia, with considerable swelling at the place of injection and the formation of a fibrinous membrane. The spleen is enlarged, and the bacteria may be found in all the internal organs and in the blood, but no specific pneumonia is developed. When **intrathoracic injections** are made in the lung substance, it produces a marked lobar pneumonia with considerable fibrinous exudate, and also symptoms of general infection. Injected in the dog intrathoracically, it may produce marked croupous pneumonia, the animal generally recovering in two or three weeks after presenting all the different stages of the disease.

II. Pneumococcus of Friedlaender (Bacillus Pneumoniæ of Fluegge).

The organism was **discovered and described** by **Friedlaender** in 1883, and believed by him to belong to the class of cocci, but recognized afterward as a bacillus. It **is found**: *a.* in a number of cases of pneumonia in the fibrinous exudate, *b.* in the blood, and *c.* in the sputum.

Morphology.—Short rods, with rounded ends, united in pairs, sometimes in fours, having a **decided capsule** when taken directly from the blood of the animal. When grown on artificial media the capsule disappears. Occasionally the capsule surrounds each individual cell, at other times it is around the cells, united in pairs or fours. This capsule may be distinctly brought out by the special method of staining capsules mentioned in the chapter on staining.

The *Bacillus pneumoniæ* **stains well** with all anilin dyes, but does not stain well by Gram's method—a diagnostic point differentiating it from the *Micrococcus pneumoniæ.*

Biologic Characters.—It is **aërobic** and **facultative anaërobic,** non-motile, and has no flagella. It grows in all the media at a temperature of between 16° and 20° C., but grows best at the temperature of the blood, 37° C. Growth ceases at a temperature exceeding 46° C. Its growth in cultures is exceedingly long lived, so that after a year or longer it has grown upon transplantation into a suitable culture.

Its growth in **bouillon** is cloudy. It does not liquefy **gelatin.** Stab-cultures in gelatin have quite a characteristic appearance, growing in the form of a nail. The head of the nail is at the point where the inoculating needle enters the gelatin, the path of the needle through the gelatin marking the body of the nail. The head of the nail is a white mass of shiny appearance; the body is opaque and made up of white spherical colonies. It produces bubbles of gas in gelatin. On gelatin plates colonies appear in twenty-four hours as small white spheres which increase rapidly in size, and in a short time on the surface of the plate large masses are formed.

Its growth on **agar** is much like that on gelatin. On **blood-serum** the growth is abundant, viscid, and grayish white in color. On potato it grows rapidly and abundantly, and is yellowish white in appearance.

Pathogenesis.—The *Bacillus pneumoniæ* is fatal to mice and guinea-pigs. Dogs and rabbits are immune. **Intrapleural injections** in susceptible animals result in a decided pleuritic effusion with formation of fibrinous membranes, intense congestion of the lungs on the injected side, great enlargement of the spleen, and general involvement of the blood (septicæmia) and internal organs; the bacillus being found everywhere.

EPIDEMIC CEREBROSPINAL MENINGITIS.

III. Diplococcus Intracellularis Meningitidis.

This organism was **discovered** by **Weichselbaum**, in 1887, in pus-cells (polymorphonuclear leucocytes) of the cerebrospinal exudate of cases of epidemic cerebrospinal meningitis.

Morphology.—The micrococcus occurs in bunches or in chains of three or four elements, the elements in the chain showing marked variation in size. **Stains** with all the anilin dyes and is **decolorized** by Gram's method. It shows marked variation of the different elements in their power of taking color; some elements being deeply stained, others scarcely at all. The organism has a low vitality; exposure in the dry state for twenty-four hours to direct sunlight at the body temperature, 37° C., is sufficient to kill it. At the room temperature it is killed in seventy-two hours when dried.

To **obtain cultures from man**, of this bacillus, what is known as **lumbar puncture of the spine** must be made. The patient is placed on the left side very much in the same position as is used for intraspinal cocainization, the skin of the patient and hands of the operator are thoroughly sterilized, and an ordinary antitoxin-serum needle is introduced into the spinal canal, between the second and third lumbar vertebræ, the skin being pierced a little to the right of the spinous process. The needle is driven in for 4 cm. in a child, and 7 to 8 cm. in an adult, until the spinal canal is reached, when the spinal fluid is allowed to drop into a clean sterilized test-tube. From 5 to 15 c.c. of fluid are generally taken for examination. Cover-glasses are prepared and a number of cultures are made. This puncture seems to be followed by no ill effect.

Biologic Characters.—This coccus is aërobic and is a **facultative saprophyte**, non-motile, has no flagella, and grows on all culture-media, but rather irregularly, thriving best on **ordinary** or **Loeffler's blood-serum.** In inoculating cultures from the exudate of patients, a large quantity of exudate must be used and a number of tubes inoculated, as otherwise no growth may be obtained. It seems to grow best when the exudate taken comes from a recent, acute case. It does not cloud **bouillon,** but causes a scanty deposit on the side and at the bottom of the fluid.

On **glycerin-agar** and **blood-serum** it grows as transparent, shiny colonies. It does not liquefy **gelatin** nor does it grow on **potato.** It grows only at the temperature of the body, 37° C., in two or three days. Cultures of this bacillus live only for five or six days, so that it is necessary to transplant them every third or fourth day.

Pathogenesis.—It can not be inoculated into animals by the ordinary methods used, but **intrameningeal injections,** either spinal or under the cerebral dura, produce a characteristic meningitis and fibrinous exudate, the bacteria invading at times the lungs, but never being found in the blood.

MALTA OR MEDITERRANEAN FEVER.

IV. Micrococcus Melitensis.

This organism was **demonstrated by** Surgeon-Major **Bruce,** of the British Army, as the **cause** of what is known as Malta or Mediterranean fever.

Morphology.—Round or oval cocci 0.5 mikron in diameter, occurring solitary or in pairs, in cultures occasionally forming chains, and **staining** by the usual anilin dyes but not by Gram's method.

The micrococcus is non-motile, but Gordon claims to have demonstrated the presence of from one to four flagella.

Biologic Characters.—It is **aërobic.** It grows very scantily on **gelatin** at 22° C. only at the end of several weeks, and does not liquefy the gelatin. It grows best in **agar,** stab cultures showing growth only at the end of several days. The colonies appear as pearly-white spots scattered around the points of puncture, and as minute round white colonies along the course of the needle-track, which increases in size, and after some weeks a rosette-shaped growth is seen upon the surface. Along the line of puncture the growth assumes a yellowish-brown color.

At 35° C. the colonies become visible only at the end of seven days; at 37° C. they are seen in three or four days.

It does not grow on **potato.**

Pathogenesis.—This micrococcus is not pathogenic for mice, guinea-pigs, or rabbits, but subcutaneous injections in monkeys have induced fever, the animal dying in from thirteen to twenty-one days. At the autopsy the spleen is found enlarged and contains the micrococcus.

In man the micrococcus is found in the enlarged spleen in great numbers.

Agglutination.—Recent cultures of *Micrococcus melitensis* are agglutinated by the blood-serum of patients suffering from Malta fever, and occasionally with some this reaction is manifested a year after recovery. This agglutinating effect has been obtained in a dilution as high as 1 in 1000.

QUESTIONS.

Give the several names of the *Micrococcus pneumoniæ;* by whom and how was it discovered?
Where is it found?
What is its morphology?
How does it stain?
How does it behave with regard to oxygen?
Does it possess flagella?
Is it motile?
In what media and at what temperature does it grow?
What is its thermal death-point?
How does it grow in bouillon, gelatin, agar, blood-serum?
What protects animals from inoculations with virulent cultures?
What animals are susceptible?
What are the effects of subcutaneous and intrathoracic injection of animals?
What is the synonym of the pneumococcus?
Is it a coccus?
By whom was it discovered?
Where is it found?
Give its morphology. Its staining properties. Give its principal bio-

PLATE II.

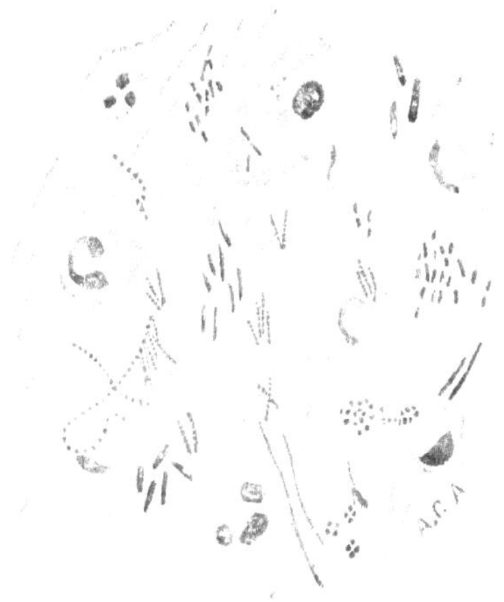

Tuberculous Sputum Stained by Gabbett's Method. Tubercle Bacilli seen as Red Rods; all else is Stained Blue. (Abbott.)

logical characters. How does it grow in bouillon, in gelatin, on agar, on blood-serum, on potato?

What animals are susceptible?

Describe the effects of subcutaneous or intrathoracic inoculations.

How is it differentiated from the preceding germ?

Where is the *Diplococcus intracellularis meningitidis* found?

By whom was it discovered?

Give its morphology, its staining properties, its principal biologic characters?

How is lumbar puncture performed?

What animals are susceptible?

How and where should the inoculation be performed?

Who discovered the *Micrococcus melitensis?*

Where was it found?

State its morphology, staining, its biologic characters.

What animals are susceptible?

In what dilution does the blood of cases of Malta fever agglutinate cultures of this micrococcus?

CHAPTER X.

TUBERCULOSIS.

Bacillus Tuberculosis.

History.—That tuberculosis, the scourge of the human race, was caused by a microörganism, had long been suspected there is no doubt, but it was not until **Koch's discovery** of the bacillus tuberculosis in 1882 that this was at all proved. (Plate II.)

Morphology.—The *Bacillus tuberculosis* is a strict parasite. It is aërobic and grows at the temperature of the human body. It is a slender rod from 1.5 to 3.5 mikrons in length, and from 0.2 to 0.5 mikron in breadth, occurring singly or in pairs united by their narrow extremities.

It is **found** in all tuberculous growths and secretions, but especially in the sputum of tuberculous patients, where its presence is the best confirmatory evidence of the existence of the disease.

Biologic Characters.—It grows with difficulty on any of the artificial media. Koch succeeded in growing it on **blood-serum.** It does not grow in **gelatin.** It thrives best on **8 per cent. glycerin-agar** or, in the mixture of Roux and

Nocard, 8 **per cent. glycerin-bouillon.** In this bouillon, kept at a temperature of 37° C., at the end of from twelve to fourteen days it forms a small pellicle on the surface.

In slant cultures of **glycerin-agar** and **blood-serum** it grows over the surface of the medium as a dried-up, scaly-looking mass. According to some authorities, it is a spore-bearing bacterium ; others fail to find the existence of spores in it. It is non-motile, though occasionally slight movements have been detected in it. It appears to have no flagella. It is usually killed by exposure to 70° C., but in the dried state may be preserved alive for a considerable time even at a temperature approaching 100° C.

Staining.—It is difficult to stain by the usual staining methods, and requires the use of special staining technic. **Koch's method** of staining it consists in adding liquor potassæ to the alkaline anilin dyes.

Ehrlich's modification of Koch's method, which consists in preparing anilin water and adding this to the solution of an anilin dye, is perhaps the best method of bringing out the tubercle bacillus.

The **mode of procedure** for the staining of bacilli in secretions, especially **in sputum,** has been described in the chapter on staining, as the **Koch-Ehrlich method,** or the **Ziehl carbol-fuchsin method,** or, better still, as **Gabbett's modification of Ziehl's method.**

In **tissue** the bacillus is stained best by an application of either method, which will also be found described in the chapter on staining.

When so stained, the bacillus shows a number of **unstained places in the cell-body,** somewhat **resembling spores.** They have given rise to the opinion that the bacilli are spore-forming, but the fact that when the usual method for staining spores is applied these spots remain unstained seems to prove that they are not spores, but are due possibly to some degeneration in the protoplasm of the bacillus.

Nature and Occurrence.—As mentioned, the tubercle bacillus is a strict parasite, and is found only in tuberculous tissues and in the secretions from tuberculous patients, especially the sputum. It is also found in substances that have been contaminated with those secretions, and occasionally are wafted in the air in this manner.

Pathogenesis.—The tubercle bacillus is pathogenic for man and for nearly all the lower animals, especially the herbivora, though the carnivora and birds are alike susceptible to it, and traces of the disease have even been found in cold-blooded animals. It may infect the whole animal economy, giving rise to local manifestations in the shape of nodules which contain the bacillus.

The usual **mode of infection** of animals is through the respiratory tract, but sometimes through the gastro-intestinal tract. Infection may occasionally be produced by the introduction of the bacilli through abrasions of the skin, as in the case of dissectors or pathologists, when it gives rise to localized tuberculous nodules on the hands, which at any time may become the source of infection of the general organism.

The usual **mode of inoculation** of animals is either by **intraperitoneal inoculation**, when it gives rise to a general tuberculosis involving especially the glands of the abdomen and the lungs, or by **subcutaneous inoculation**, when a small quantity of the culture or a small bit of the suspected substance is used.

The **usual contaminating substance** for man is the **secretion of tuberculous patients**, which may be deposited on utensils used by others, or which through carelessness may have dried in the room, thus contaminating the dust of the apartment, which, wafted through the air, is brought into contact with the mucous membrane of the respiratory organs of susceptible individuals. In this way the air of hospital wards of consumptives and the various articles of furniture in rooms inhabited by consumptives have been proved to be infectious.

The **drinking of contaminated milk** and the eating of meat from tuberculous animals are believed in some instances to have spread the disease. This, however, is not thoroughly proved, and recently the eminent Koch has asserted that this mode of contamination is exceedingly rare, and is an equation which in the treatment and the prevention of tuberculosis may be altogether neglected.

It has been assumed that human, avian, and bovine tuberculosis are identical. In a remarkable paper on tuberculosis by Koch, read before the Tuberculosis Congress in 1901, at Berlin, he denies this identity, and shows by a number of experiments that cattle can not be inoculated with the secretion of tuberculous patients, and that man is not affected by eating meat from contaminated oxen.

As regards the **transmission of tuberculosis,** the part played by heredity is almost *nil.* It has failed of demonstration that fœtuses or young children from intensely tuberculous mothers have in their secretions or tissues the tubercle bacillus; and reasoning by analogy, as in Bang's method, the separation of newborn calves from their tuberculous mothers has completely succeeded in eliminating tuberculous diseases from these calves, it must be assumed that like precautions would produce identical results in man.

The **tubercle bacilli secrete a poisonous material,** which is chiefly contained in the bacterial cells themselves, and is known by the name of **tuberculin.** This tuberculin is believed to be a preventative against tubercular diseases; and in 1890 Koch proclaimed that by means of injections of this substance he had succeeded in curing tuberculosis. This promise has not been fully realized, but Koch's discovery has given us valuable information, and has demonstrated that by injection of this tuberculin healthy animals may be recognized and so separated from tuberculous ones long before the disease could be diagnosed in the latter by physical signs; for the former are not affected by small doses of tuberculin, whereas animals that have the least tuberculous taint will show decided reaction when injected with tuberculin. This procedure is used extensively in all civilized countries nowadays for the diagnosis of tuberculosis in cattle and other animals.

The **original tuberculin of Koch is prepared** from an extract of glycerin-bouillon of virulent bacteria, in which the bacteria themselves are quickly killed by exposure to a higher temperature, and filtered away by a Chamberlain filter. 0.025

c.c. of such an extract will in tuberculous animals develop marked reactionary symptoms, whereas when used in healthy animals it gives rise to no reaction.

This tuberculin has a **beneficial action in man,** especially an action on local tuberculous diseases, such as lupus, tuberculous joints, etc. It is dangerous, however, when used therapeutically, because it shows a tendency to stimulate the development of dormant tuberculosis.

Recently **different forms of tuberculin** have been prepared by Koch, known as tuberculin A, O, and R.

Tuberculin A.—This is **prepared** by extracting the bacilli with decinormal salt solution, and acts very much like ordinary tuberculin, being even more severe in effect.

Tuberculin O.—This is **prepared** by pounding the dried tubercle bacilli and extracting with distilled water, the emulsion being then passed through the centrifuge. The residue after centrifugation is dried and again pounded and extracted with water, and these processes repeated until no solid residue is left. The whitish liquids from all these operations are mixed, and the result is **tuberculin R.**

Tuberculin O is identical in effect to tuberculin A and has an immunizing effect. **Tuberculin R** gives rise to little reaction, but has a decided immunizing effect. The fluid in tuberculin R is made so that 1 c.c. corresponds to 10 milligrams of solid matter, and must be diluted with sterile salt solution to bring it to the required strength. In applying the same therapeutically the dose of tuberculin R for an adult is $\frac{1}{500}$ to 1 milligram. It must be used hypodermatically, and should be administered every other day. The dose should not give rise to a temperature exceeding 1 degree C.

This produces very satisfactory results in the treatment of lupus, but so far in tuberculous diseases of the lung its effects have not come up to expectation.

Recently, the tubercle bacillus, on account of its peculiar growth in some cases in which it seems to present projecting processes or branches, has been thought by some to belong to the higher bacteria, being probably a streptothrix, closely related to the actinomyces.

QUESTIONS.

When and by whom was the *Bacillus tuberculosis* discovered? How does the bacillus behave in the presence of oxygen?

What is the size of the tubercle bacillus? In what tissues and secretions of tuberculous animals is it usually found? How is it best artificially grown? What temperature is most favorable for its growth? How high a temperature does it resist?

Give two methods of staining the tubercle bacillus in cultures or in the secretions of animals. Give the mode of staining the bacteria in tissue? What has given rise to the idea of spores in the bacillus?

What animals besides man are the most susceptible to tuberculous diseases? What two forms of infection follow inoculation of this bacillus? What is the usual mode of infection in man?

Mention some cases of localized tuberculosis in man. How are animals inoculated to produce the disease? What are the usual infecting agents in man?

What part does tuberculous milk or tuberculous meat play in the dissemination of tuberculosis?

What was the subject of Koch's paper at the Congress of Tuberculosis, in 1901?

What part does heredity play in the transmission of tuberculosis?

What is tuberculin?

What diagnostic purpose does tuberculin serve?

How is tuberculin prepared?

What is meant by Tuberculin A, O, and R?

Why has the tubercle bacillus been thought to be a streptothrix?

CHAPTER XI.

LEPROSY AND SYPHILIS.

LEPROSY.

Bacillus Lepræ.

History.—The specific cause of leprosy is a bacillus known as the *Bacillus lepræ*, **discovered** by **Hansen**, and **confirmed** by **Neisser**, in 1879.

The bacillus **is found** *a.* in the tissues of leprous patients, and *b.* in the secretions, with the exception of the urine. It has never been found in the blood.

Morphology.—The bacilli are small straight rods with pointed ends, sometimes curved, measuring from 5 to 6 mikrons in length, non-motile, resembling very much the tubercle bacillus, but are more uniform in length and not so frequently bent. When stained, their protoplasm shows unstained spaces similar to those of the tubercle bacillus, which are regarded by some as spores.

Biology.—Bordoni-Uffreduzzi claims to have cultivated the bacillus through a number of generations in **glycerinized gelatin.** Byron (*Researches Loomis Laboratory*, 1892) made a pure culture of the bacillus on **agar.**

From the secretions and scrapings obtained from an ulcer of the nares in a leper the author found upon examination a great many bacilli lying in cells, some cells containing as many as 3 or 4 bunches, and was able to procure a pure culture on **Loeffler's blood-serum** and **glycerin-agar.**

The growth upon the serum very much resembled a twisted band of yellowish-gray color, and developed very rapidly at 37° C. Cultures in **bouillon** and **potato** did not develop.

The *Bacillus lepræ* **stains** very readily with the anilin dyes, and also by Gram's method. It very greatly resembles the tubercle bacillus in retaining its color when subsequently treated with strong solutions of mineral acids.

An interesting point about the staining of the *Bacillus lepræ* which will permit **differentiation from the Bacillus tuberculosis** is that the lepra bacillus is rapidly stained by the Gram method, while the tubercle bacillus stains with great difficulty by it, and must remain at least twenty-four hours in the color dish before taking the stain.

Baumgarten's differentiation between these two bacteria is to subject cover-glass preparations which have been smeared with scrapings from leprous nodules or ulcers for five minutes in the Ehrlich solution, and afterward to decolorize with solution of nitric acid in alcohol, 1 part of acid to 10 parts of alcohol. The bacillus of Hansen will be stained, while the tubercle bacillus will not.

A number of investigators have by **inoculation** with fresh extirpated leprous tissue succeeded in reproducing the disease in the lower animals. Tedeschi inoculated a monkey **under the dura mater,** and death resulted in six days. Many lepra bacilli were found in the spleen and spinal cord at the autopsy.

Nature of Leprosy.—Besnier, with many others, contends that leprosy is a bacterial disease exclusively limited to man, and that the microörganisms will reproduce themselves in man alone, and not in animals.

Dyer, from observation of leprosy in fifty cases in Louisiana, concludes positively that the direct cause of the disease is the lepra bacillus. The indirect cause is contagion. The disease therefore is not hereditary.

A very **useful method of diagnosis** for physicians who wish to make a speedy and positive proof of leprosy, and have no microtome or laboratory facilities, is to remove a bit of skin or scraping near a tubercle or nodule and place the same in a mortar with some saline solution and triturate until a homogeneous solution results, adding from time to time enough saline solution to prevent drying. A small quantity of this emulsion is transferred to a clean cover-glass, air-dried, and fixed over a flame, stained with the Ziehl carbol-fuchsin for five minutes, then washed in water, counterstained, and decolorized with Gabbett's solution of methylene-blue and sulphuric acid for two minutes, washed again in water, dried, and mounted in Canada balsam. The bacilli will appear red, while the rest of the tissue will be stained blue.

SYPHILIS.

Bacillus of Syphilis.

History.—In 1884–1885 **Lustgarten** described a bacillus which he had discovered in the primary sore and secondary manifestations of syphilis. Rarely could this bacillus be found in the tertiary stages of the disease.

In **size** and **shape** the bacillus very closely resembles that of tuberculosis, but differs from it especially in its **cultural peculiarities** and also in its **staining properties** with the anilin dyes. For instance, the bacillus could not be cultivated on any of the artificial media, not even on those on which the *Bacillus tuberculosis* could be made to grow; and in staining the *Bacillus syphilidis* it showed considerable difficulty in taking up the anilin colors, yet when stained according to Ehrlich's or Ziehl's method it very quickly parted with its colors when washed in mineral acids, especially sulphuric acid, contrary to what happens in the case of the *Bacillus tuberculosis*. When decolorized, however, by means of alcohol the *Bacillus syphilidis* retained the dye for a considerable time.

For the **staining of sections** the following method is recommended: Place the section in a cold solution of anilin-water gentian-violet for from twelve to twenty-four hours at the room temperature, or for two hours at a temperature of 40° C. Wash a few minutes in absolute alcohol, then put the section for some seconds into 1.5 per cent. solution of permanganate of potassium, pass rapidly (for one or two seconds) into sulphuric acid solution, wash thoroughly in water, and mount on xylol balsam. When stained by this method the *Bacillus syphilidis* shows considerable resemblance to the *Bacillus tuberculosis*, being of similar size and showing similar refractive spots in the body of the cell.

As mentioned above, this bacillus has not been successfully cultivated artificially, and inoculations of animals have also been barren of results.

Streptococcus of Syphilis.

Vanniessen, by collecting blood of syphilitic subjects, and allowing same to coagulate in sterilized tubes, has been able from the serum of this blood to cultivate a streptococcus which he believes to be the etiological factor in syphilis. His experiments, however, have failed of confirmation by others.

QUESTIONS.

When and by whom was the *Bacillus lepræ* found? Where is it found?

Describe the *Bacillus lepræ*. Does it contain spores? How is it grown artificially? How does it stain?

How do you differentiate *Bacillus lepræ* from the *Bacillus tuberculosis* by staining? What animals are susceptible to the infection?

Give a ready method for the diagnosis of a leprous ulcer or nodule, and give a diagnosis of leprosy in a suspected case.

Describe the *Bacillus syphilidis* of Lustgarten? Where is it found? How does it stain? How decolorized? How does it stain in tissue? How does it grow in artificial culture-media?

Differentiate between *Bacillus syphilidis* and *Bacillus tuberculosis*.

CHAPTER XII.

GLANDERS (FARCY).

Bacillus Mallei.

GLANDERS is a disease of the horse and ass tribe, **characterized** by the formation of nodules in the mucous membrane of the mouth and respiratory passages. These nodules, very prone to ulcerate, give rise to profuse suppuration, and very soon afterward the lymphatic glands of the neck begin to enlarge. These glands soften early and discharge a very virulent pus. Secondarily the lungs become infected, the infectious material forming small nodules very much resembling tubercles in appearance.

History.—In 1882, **Loeffler discovered** in the discharges and tissues of animals affected with this disease a specific microorganism which he called *Bacillus mallei.*

Morphology.—Glanders bacillus is a bacillus with rounded or pointed ends, occurring generally singly, occasionally in pairs, seldom or never forming threads. The bacillus is nonmotile, and therefore possesses no flagella.

Spores.—Some observers claim to have discovered spores in the glanders bacillus, but, reasoning by analogy, those shiny particles described as spores are really not spores; they are the same as the shiny particles discovered in stained preparations of the *Bacillus tuberculosis,* and they cannot be stained by the usual methods of spore-staining, nor do the bacteria containing same resist conditions which are usually resisted by other spore-bearing bacteria. The observation of Loeffler, however, that this microörganism is able to grow after being kept in the dry state for a long time, makes it appear as if some form of permanent spore existed.

Biology.—The *Bacillus mallei* grows readily on all ordinary media at a temperature between 25° and 38° C. Its growth is very slow, and on this account its isolation and cultivation by the usual plate-methods are rather difficult. Upon **nutrient agar** it appears as a moist opaque layer. On **gelatin** its growth is much less voluminous than on agar. It does not liquefy the gelatin. In **blood-serum** the growth is opaque, moist, of a bright-yellow color; the serum is not liquefied. On **potato** at 37° C. its growth is rapid, moist, and of an amber-yellow color, which becomes darker with age and finally becomes of a reddish-brown. It causes clouding of **bouillon**, with a tenacious, ropy sediment. In **litmus milk** it produces acidity

FIG. 52.

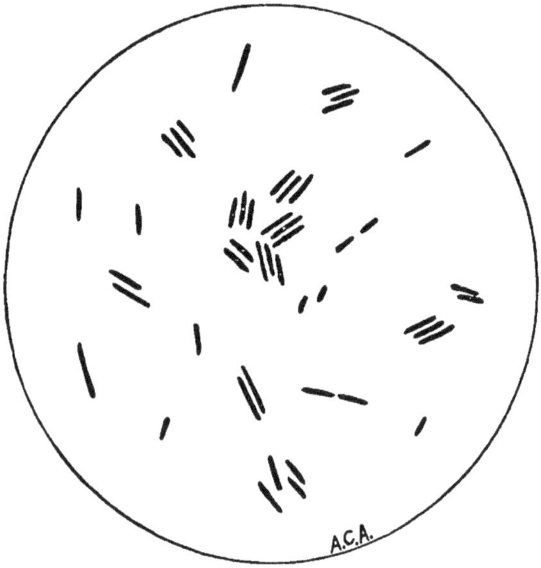

Bacillus of glanders (*Bacillus mallei*), from culture. (Abbott.)

in four or five days, as seen by the change of color from blue to red. It also causes coagulation of the milk.

Bacillus mallei is very susceptible to the effect of high temperature. At 40° C. it will grow for twenty or more days. It will not grow at 43° C., and if exposed to that temperature for forty-eight hours it is destroyed. It is killed by a temperature of 50° C. in five hours, and does not survive more than five minutes at a temperature of 55° C. It is **aërobic** and **facultative anaërobic.**

It **stains** readily with all the anilin dyes, but presents in its body conspicuous irregularity of staining, showing places stained very deeply and others that have scarcely any dye at all.

It is difficult to **stain in tissues** from the fact that, though readily stained, the bacillus parts very quickly with its coloring-matter in the presence of a decolorizing agent, and even in the alcohol used to dehydrate the tissue.

A number of **methods for staining sections of tissue** for the bacillus of glanders have been suggested. The following is the best:

Transfer the sections from alcohol to distilled water, put the sections upon a slide and absorb the water with blotting-paper, stain for a half-hour with a few drops of a 10 per cent. solution of carbol-fuchsin in water, remove the superfluous stain with blotting-paper, wash the sections three times in a 0.3 per cent. acetic acid solution, not allowing the acid to act more than ten seconds each time, and remove the acid by carefully washing with distilled water. Absorb all water with blotting-paper, and heat moderately over the flame so as to drive off the remaining water. Clear in xylol and mount in xylol balsam. In properly stained tissues the bacilli will be found more numerous in the centre of the nodule, becoming fewer as the periphery is approached.

The **animals susceptible** to **infection by glanders**, besides horses and asses, are guinea-pigs, cats, and field-mice. The rabbit is very little so; dogs and sheep still less so. Man is susceptible, and not seldom the infection terminates fatally. House-mice, rats, cattle, and hogs are insusceptible.

For **inoculation experiments** the guinea-pig is made use of. The experiment is generally performed by **subcutaneous** inoculation of the culture or a small piece of the nodule from the diseased animal. The most prominent **symptom** in the animal is the enlargement of the spleen, with formation of nodules in that organ and in the liver. From these nodules the glanders bacillus may be obtained in pure culture. The animals live from six to eight weeks. The specific character of the inflammation of the mucous membrane of the nostrils is almost always present. The joints become swollen and the testicles enormously distended; the internal organs—lungs, kidney, spleen, and liver—are the seats of the nodular deposits, from which bacilli may be obtained in pure cultures.

Diagnosis.—The method of Strauss for the recognition of the disease is of great importance clinically. With it in a short time a diagnosis may be arrived at, while by the ordinary methods of inoculation it would take weeks to come to a certain conclusion. Its details are these: Into the peritoneal cavity of a *male* guinea-pig a bit of the suspected tissue is introduced. If the case be one of glanders, in about thirty hours the testicles begin to swell and the skin covering them becomes red and shining, and there is evidence of abscess-formation. *The tumefaction of the testicle is a true diagnostic sign.*

Mallein, the toxic principle secreted by the bacillus, has been isolated from **old glycerin-bouillon** cultures of the *Bacillus mallei.* For this purpose the cultures are steamed in a sterilizer for several hours and then filtrated through a Chamberlain porcelain filter and evaporated to one-tenth of their volume.

This mallein is **used as a diagnostic test** for glanders in animals, very much as tuberculin is for tuberculosis. It produces when injected in very small quantity a rise of a degree and a half C. if the animal be at all infected with the disease, but in healthy animals injection is followed by no febrile reaction.

Some observers have asserted that the injection of this mallein into susceptible animals will protect them from the disease; other observers assert that the blood-serum of naturally immune animals is curative when injected into infected animals. But these points are not fully determined.

QUESTIONS.

What are the synonyms for the bacillus of glanders?
What are the symptoms of glanders in the horse?
By whom and when was this bacillus discovered?
Describe the bacillus.
Does it contain spores?
Give reasons for and against its spore-formation.

What are its cultural peculiarities, if any, on agar, on gelatin, on potato, on blood-serum, in bouillon, in litmus milk?

Give a method of staining the glanders bacillus in tissue.

Give the method of inoculation of a guinea-pig, and the prominent symptoms.

How long does the animal live?

Give Strauss' method of inoculation for diagnosis.

What is mallein? How is it obtained? What are its uses? Does it protect from glanders?

CHAPTER XIII.

ANTHRAX.

Bacillus Anthracis.

History.—The *Bacillus anthracis*, **discovered** and described by **Davaine**, in 1868, is the first bacillus that was demonstrated to be pathogenic to man and animals.

It is **found in** the blood and tissues of animals which have died of this disease, which is known as **splenic fever,** and **charbon.**

It produces in these animals a genuine septicæmia, the capillaries all over the body teeming with the microörganisms.

No bacteria have more than the *Bacillus anthracis* helped to establish the **three postulates of Koch** used in testing the pathogenicity of bacteria. These postulates are as follows:

I. **For a microörganism to be considered the cause of a disease,** it must at all times be found in the organs, blood, or secretions of an animal dead or affected with the disease.

II. It must be possible to **isolate this organism and obtain it in pure cultures** from the same sources. It may also be grown for several generations in artificial culture-media.

III. **Inoculation of these pure cultures into susceptible animals** must give rise to the same symptoms and changes found in the animal originally affected, and the same bacteria must be found in their blood, tissues, or secretions.

Morphology.—The anthrax bacillus is a rod bacterium measuring from 2 to 3 mikrons when found in the blood and tissues of animals; from 20 to 25 mikrons when obtained from cultures; and of a uniform thickness of 1.25 mikrons. The ends of the rod seem a little thicker than the rest of the body, and under a low power look square, but with a higher power they are seen to be concave (Fig. 53).

FIG. 53.

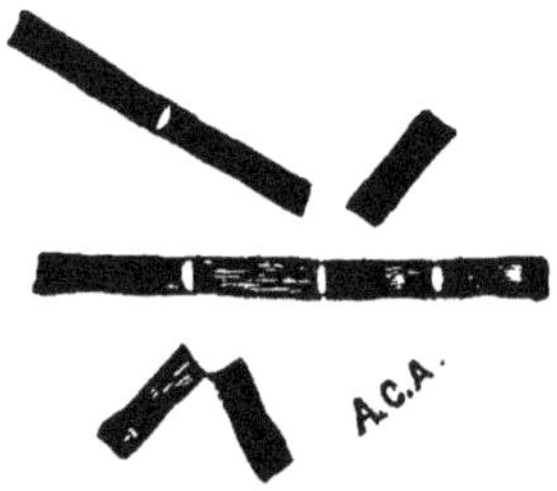

Bacillus anthracis, highly magnified to show swellings and concavities at extremities of the single cells. (Abbott.)

It is found singly or in pairs in the blood and tissues of diseased animals, but when cultivated in bouillon or in the hanging drop it forms long threads which may or may not contain spores.

It is **stained** by all the alkaline anilin dyes, the spores

FIG. 54.

Threads of *Bacillus anthracis* containing spores. × about 1200. (Abbott.)

remaining uncolored; but the latter are easily stained by any of the special methods for staining spores described in the chapter on staining.

Biologic Characters.—The *Bacillus anthracis* is **anaërobic,** but can grow without the presence of oxygen. When grown with free access of oxygen in artificial culture-media it forms long filaments or threads, which are formed by the union of a number of bacilli. In the presence of free oxygen elliptical bright spots, one to each segment of the thread, are observed; these are the spores.

This bacillus grows at all temperatures between 12° and 45° C., but it does not form spores at a temperature below 18° or above 42° C. Its maximum of growth is at 37.5° C. (Fig. 54).

In the blood and tissues of animals it does not sporulate. The bacterium is non-motile and has no flagella.

In **bouillon** it grows very rapidly, forming twisted thread-like masses, resembling cotton, in the mass of the bouillon

FIG. 55.

Colony of *Bacillus anthracis* on agar-agar. (Abbott.)

and at the bottom of the tube, but it does not cloud the medium.

On **agar** its growth is quite characteristic, forming colonies which look like irregularly twisted knots of thread resembling cotton-wool; this peculiar growth has been given the name of the head of Medusa (Fig. 55).

On **gelatin** its growth is very like that on agar, but it liquefies the medium. On **potato** it grows rapidly as a dull white, thread-like mass.

Resistance to Thermal Changes.—It does not grow at a temperature below 12° C. or above 45° C. It may, however, **when containing spores**, be kept for almost an indefinite period even when dried and exposed to a high temperature, and be subsequently grown when brought in a suitable medium. The spores resist a freezing temperature, and even the temperature of liquid air, for almost an indefinite time. They are killed by dry heat at a temperature of 140° C. only after three hours' exposure, and at 150° C. only after one hour's exposure. By moist heat at the temperature of 100° C. they are killed in from three to four minutes. They resist the action of 5 per cent. carbolic acid for five minutes.

Its **non-sporing forms** are killed by a temperature of 54° C.

Pathogenesis.—Cattle, sheep, horses, mice, guinea-pigs, and rabbits are all susceptible to the action of the bacilli. Amphibia, dogs, white rats, and birds are not susceptible. Susceptible animals may be infected in one of four ways: through the abrasions of the skin and mucous surfaces, through the respiratory tract, through the alimentary tract, or by subcutaneous inoculation, as generally practised in the laboratory.

When the bacillus is **inoculated subcutaneously** into animals, the animal shows little or no inflammation at the point of inoculation, but marked œdema of the subcutaneous tissue at a distance from the inoculating point, with small points of blood extravasation in this tissue. To the naked eye there is very little change in the internal organs except in the spleen, which is enlarged, darker, and soft. Bacilli may be found everywhere in the capillaries, in organs and blood, but especially in the vessels of the lungs, the liver, and in the glomeruli of the kidneys. Death takes place in from one to three days according to the size of the animal and the dose given.

The most susceptible animal is the mouse, next comes the guinea-pig, and then the rabbit, and so uniformly is the resistance of these animals shown to the action of inoculations with anthrax that the virulence of attenuated cultures used for protective inoculations are tested on those animals.

Immunization.—Pasteur has demonstrated that attenuated cultures of the *Bacillus anthracis* when injected into susceptible animals are capable of protecting the same against the action of the virulent bacillus, subsequently inoculated, and against an attack of the disease itself. His inoculation or vaccination consists in using cultures that have been attenuated by means of heat. For that purpose the bacteria are cultivated in large Erlenmeyer flasks at a temperature of between 42° and 43° C., for a period of time varying from ten to thirty days, when they do not form spores. The pathogenic power of these cultures is tested every few days on guinea-pigs and rabbits, and when a small dose of the culture will kill a mouse and a guinea-pig, but fails to kill a rat, it is called **vaccine No. 2.** In a few days more this same culture will fail to kill a guinea-pig, but will still kill a mouse; it is then **vaccine No. 1.**

In **veterinary practice** large animals, as sheep, cattle, and horses, are inoculated with aseptic precautions with 3 c.c. of vaccine No. 1. Then they show little or no reaction. In ten days or two weeks more they are inoculated with vaccine No. 2, when they again show some little reaction ; and a few days after this second vaccination they are able to withstand an inoculation of virulent cultures of the bacilli. This mode of vaccination has been of inestimable value by making it possible to stop the ravages of epidemics of anthrax. It is practised extensively in countries like France, Germany, and Russia, where the disease is very prevalent among sheep and cattle. In the Southern States the author has had occasion to use it extensively during the last few years, with decided benefit.

The **manner of infection** among animals with the bacilli has not been fully demonstrated. It seems to occur in the majority of cases from the soil, possibly from the fact that animals which have died of the disease have been buried too near the surface. It is therefore advisable that animals dead from anthrax be buried at a depth not less than six feet from the surface, as the soil at that depth is 15° C. even in summer. Consequently the bacilli developed in the dead bodies so buried, both on account of the low temperature of the soil and of the deprivation of oxygen, will not form spores and are not likely therefore to survive for any length of time.

QUESTIONS.

Where and by whom was the *Bacillus anthracis* first discovered?
What are the three postulates of Koch?
Describe the anthrax bacillus?
How does it stain?
How does it appear in the blood of animals? How in culture-media?
When does it form spores?
How does it grow on gelatin? How on agar? How on potato?
At what temperature does it grow?
When does it cease to form spores?
Are spores found in the animal body?
How resistant are the spores?
In what four ways are animals injected?
How are animals inoculated?
Describe the lesions found in animals after subcutaneous inoculation?
How are cultures attenuated to prepare the anthrax vaccine?
What is vaccine No. 1? Vaccine No. 2?
How is protecting vaccination practised?

CHAPTER XIV.

DIPHTHERIA AND PSEUDODIPHTHERIA.

DIPHTHERIA.

Bacillus Diphtheriæ.

History.—The **infectious nature of diphtheria** had been suspected for a long time when **Klebs** in 1883, and later **Loeffler** in 1884, discovered and accurately described in the false membranes of diphtheritic patients the presence of a microorganism which bears their combined name—Klebs-Loeffler. Indeed, no infectious disease has been better studied from its etiological and therapeutical standpoints than diphtheria, and it conforms absolutely to the postulates of Koch before mentioned: that is, it is found in animals sick with the disease, it may be cultivated artificially, and pure cultures inoculated into susceptible animals produce the disease. The disease is not produced by any other germs, and besides injection of its toxins produces in animals substances which are of immunizing value when injected into susceptible animals.

The *Bacillus diphtheriæ* **is found** *a.* in false membranes of diphtheritic origin ; *b.* occasionally in the mouth and nose of healthy individuals ; and *c.* in the dust of rooms inhabited by diphtheritic patients, or on articles of clothing or furniture which, though they may not have come into direct contact with the patients, yet have been in the same room with them.

Morphology.—The Klebs-Loeffler bacillus is a short rod, from 2 to 6 mikrons in length, and from 0.2 to 0.8 mikron in breadth, being found longer in certain cultures than in others, and when grown for several generations in artificial media. The rods occur singly or in pairs, or in irregular groups ; they may be straight or sometimes slightly curved. Occasionally one or both of the extremities are thicker than the rest of the body of the cell ; at other times the centre of the cell bulges and the end of the cell tapers (Figs. 56, 57, 58).

FIG. 56.

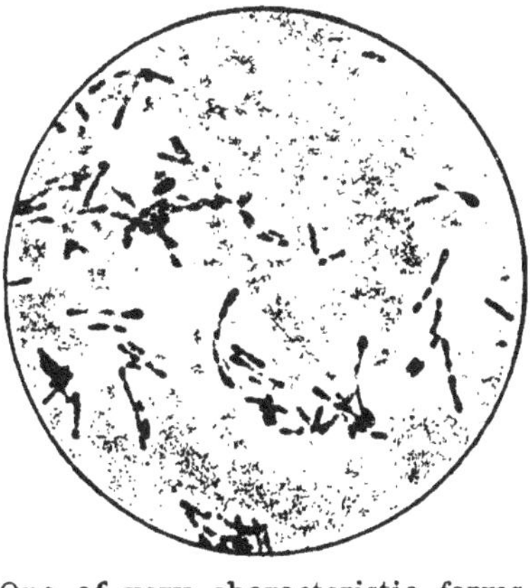

One of very characteristic forms of diphtheria bacilli from blood-serum cultures, showing clubbed ends and irregular stain. × 1100. Stain, methylene-blue. (Park.)

FIG. 57.

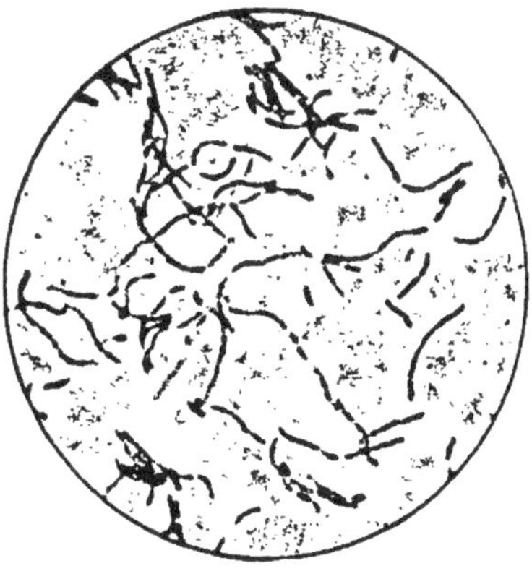

Extremely long form of diphtheria bacillus. This culture has grown on artificial media for four years and produces strong toxin. × 1100. (Park.)

Bacillus diphtheriæ **stains** with all of the anilin dyes and by Gram's method, but better with Loeffler's alkaline methylene-blue solution. For the purpose of differentiation the Neisser special stain is often used.

The bacilli cells do not stain uniformly ; they contain large granules, occasionally situated at one or both extremities or in its central portion, which stain much more deeply than the rest of the cells, and which make of a stained diphtheria preparation quite a characteristic picture under the microscope.

Neisser's Differential Method.—Some forms of false diphtheria bacilli which can not be separated from diphtheria

FIG. 58.

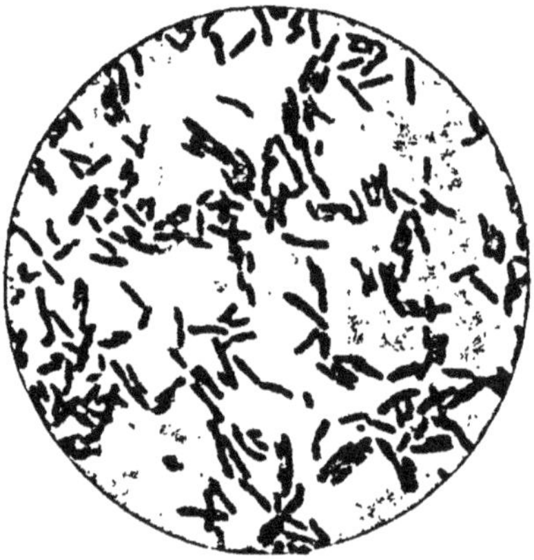

Diphtheria bacilli characteristic in shape but showing even staining. In appearance similar to the xerosis bacillus. × 1100. Stain, methylene-blue.

bacilli by their mode of growth or by their appearance under the microscope, but which are not toxic, must be differentiated from the toxin-producing bacilli; and Neisser has suggested the following method, which is used in a number of municipal laboratories. It consists of two solutions, as follows:

Solution No. 1.

Alcohol (96 per cent.),	20 parts;
Methylene-blue,	1 part;
Distilled water,	950 parts;
Glacial acetic acid,	50 parts;

Solution No. 2.

Bismarck-brown,	1 part;
Hot distilled water,	500 parts.

Put a cover-glass prepared in the usual way for two or three seconds into No. 1; then pass into No. 2 and let it remain there for three to five seconds; wash, air-dry, mount in balsam. The body of the bacteria will be stained brown, and the usually darkly stained granules with the Loeffler method will be stained blue. *If the bacilli under examination are true diphtheria bacilli, the majority of them will show the blue granule. If the bacilli are pseudodiphtheritic bacilli, scarcely any or few will show a blue stain in their interior.*

Biologic Characters.—The *Bacillus diphtheriæ* is **aërobic,** but can grow in the presence of oxygen, and is therefore a **facultative anaërobic**; it is non-motile, has no flagella, does not form spores, and does not liquefy gelatin.

Its **thermal death-point** is 58° C. It grows at ordinary room temperature, but slowly. Its maximum of growth is between 37° and 38° C. It is easily killed by disinfectants. Exposure to direct sunlight destroys the bacilli in a few days. In albuminous fluid and in the dark it may live, even when dried, for months. It grows on all artificial culture-media, but best in **blood-serum** prepared after the formula of Loeffler, a modification of which, employed in many municipal laboratories, is as follows:

Blood-serum from sheep or calves,	3 parts;
Peptone-bouillon containing 1 per cent. of glucose,	1 part.

Mix, distribute among test-tubes, sterilize, and harden by exposing in a slanting position in a steam sterilizer at 97° C. for two hours.

On this mixture at 37° C. after twelve hours the colonies are round, grayish-white, about the size of a pin-head; later they become larger, elevated, and yellowish, with the centre more opaque than the periphery. At the end of a few days the colonies have a diameter of from 3 to 5 millimeters.

In **bouillon** at 37° C. the cultures present small clots deposited on the side and at the bottom of the tube. Some of the culture floats on the surface of the liquid, forming a thin whitish pellicle. The bouillon, which is at first cloudy, becomes in a few days clear, and remains so. The sugars contained in the bouillon are fermented, and it is due to their fermentation that this medium has at first a tendency to be acid; but subsequently, when the fermentation is complete, become decidedly more alkaline. On **gelatin** the colonies develop very slowly. They appear white, round, irregularly notched, and somewhat granular, never attaining a large size. On **agar** the growth presents the same characteristics as on blood-serum; but on the surface of agar plates the colonies are quite characteristic, having a dark elevated centre and flat periphery, with a radiated appearance and indented edges. On **potato** the growth is invisible at first; and at the end of several days a thin whitish veil seems to cover the portion of the potato which has been inoculated. In **milk** it grows at a temperature as low as 20° C., without any appreciable change of the medium.

Pathogenesis.—Diphtheria, along with tetanus, should be classified among the toxic diseases. As a matter of fact, the symptoms met with in cases of diphtheria are due to the effects of the **toxins secreted by the bacilli**; very few, if any, of the microörganisms are ever found in the blood or deep-seated organs in cases of this disease; and filtered cultures from which the bacilli have been completely eliminated, when inoculated into animals give rise to symptoms identical with those induced by inoculation of the virulent bacilli themselves. Roux and Yersin, by the filtration of cultures through unglazed porcelain, have been able to separate from the bacilli a **toxalbumin** which, when injected under the skin of rabbits and guinea-pigs, produces the blood-poisoning, renal and nervous symptoms met with in pure diphtheria. Welch and Abbott have repeated these experiments, and having established the same facts have come to the same conclusion as to the action of this toxalbumin.

Subcutaneous inoculations of the diphtheria bacilli will produce death in guinea-pigs in about thirty-six hours. The following lesions are found at the autopsy: General œdema at the point of inoculation, with the formation of a false membrane. Marked congestion of the adrenal bodies, serous or serosanguinolent effusions in the pleural cavities, and swollen spleen. A few of the bacilli may be found at the point of inoculation and in the fluid of the œdema. In the blood and internal organs no bacilli can be found, showing that the symptoms are purely toxic.

Roux and Yersin have also been able to produce the false membrane giving rise to the disease, by the inoculation of rabbits and guinea-pigs into the mucous surfaces or into the skin, and they have reproduced in animals the characteristic diphtheria paralysis. This paralysis, best seen in the rabbit, usually begins in the posterior extremities and gradually extends over the whole body, death being caused by paralysis of the heart and respiratory organs.

Different cultures of diphtheria bacilli, though emanating from equally virulent cases of diphtheria, and grown under the same conditions, show at times a **great variation in toxicity.** The explanation of this has not been as yet satisfactorily given. But this fact we should remember when testing the efficacy of antitoxins in neutralizing the toxins of diphtheria.

Diphtheria Diagnosis.—Clinically it is not always easy to differentiate diphtheria in its early stages from other affections of the throat and nose which are characterized by the presence of exudates. *In view of the recent therapeutical advances in diphtheria, it is important that a very early diagnosis be made.* For this purpose, accepting the almost unanimous opinions of experts, that diphtheria is due to the presence of diphtheria bacilli in the membranous exudate, boards of health, cities, and hospitals have established a **diphtheria service** for the purpose of facilitating the early recognition of the disease. In order to carry out this method, a **central laboratory with all facilities** is established, and in cities a number of **supply-depots** are located within reach of the practising physician, where the material in **complete outfits** necessary to make cultures from the throats of suspected cases of diphtheria may be procured. These outfits consist of a **blood-serum culture-tube** (Fig. 59) made after the formula of Loeffler, and a **swab** or **applicator** kept in a well-sterilized test-tube. This swab is a small iron rod roughened on one of its ends, and on which a little absorbent cotton is twisted. The test-tube containing the swab is plugged with absorbent cotton and then thoroughly sterilized by dry heat for one hour at 150° C. The blood-serum and swab are neatly packed together in a small pasteboard or wooden box, together with a blank form giving instructions as to how to make the cultures.

The **cultures from the throat are made as follows:**

The patient is put in the best possible light, and if he is a child is held firmly by an assistant, the mouth is opened, the

FIG. 59.

Culture-box used in municipal laboratories to prepare cultures from throats of diphtheria suspects.

tongue depressed by means of a spoon or other instrument, the swab taken out of its containing tube and gently rubbed over the false membrane or exudate in the throat, if any, or if no false membrane be present, over the surface of the pillar of the fauces, after which, without laying down the swab, the serum-tube is taken, the plug of cotton removed, and the surface of the swab which has been in contact with the throat of the patient is gently and freely rubbed over the surface of the blood-serum, being careful not to break into it, and certain to rub all sides of the swab upon the serum. After which the swab is returned to its tube, both tubes plugged, and the whole outfit with the blank form filled in is returned to the laboratory. On receiving the tube at the laboratory it is incubated at a temperature of 37° C. for twelve hours, at the end of which time it is ready for examination. If the case is one of diphtheria, the typical diphtheria growth is found on the surface of the culture. This consists of grayish or yellowish-white glistening spots, and a cover-glass preparation made of these shows in typical cases the Klebs-Loeffler bacillus, as short, thick rods, with rounded edges, irregular in shape, showing a decided staining in some parts of their body, deficient in color in other parts, and characterized chiefly by the variety of form of the different bacteria forming the culture.

In exceptional cases it is possible to find colonies as early as five or six hours after incubation.

Indeed, for cases outside of the city limits, in the municipal laboratory in New Orleans, it has been possible to make examinations of the swabs themselves by making cover-glass preparations from the same even two or three days after they were prepared, and in a great majority of the cases come to a positive or negative conclusion, verified later clinically and also bacteriologically, by cultures made from these same swabs.

It is essential for these examinations that the cultures from the throats of suspected cases be made before antiseptics have been applied to the throat, or, if that is not possible, the cultures should be made at an interval of at least two or three hours after such applications, as otherwise the antiseptics may have acted on the bacilli on the surface of the membrane and destroyed them or greatly inhibited their growth.

PSEUDODIPHTHERIA.

Bacillus Pseudodiphtheriæ.

Another source of error in the application of this method comes from the pseudodiphtheria bacilli which are found in cultures, and which greatly resemble the virulent *Bacillus diphtheriæ*, but have no pathogenic power.

These pseudobacilli are of **two kinds**:

I. It is not possible to separate the first kind from the true diphtheria bacilli either by morphology or cultural properties. When **injected** into the lower animals they are non-virulent, because they **secrete no toxin.**

II. The second kind, in the opinion of the author, are very improperly so-called, for they are not diphtheria bacilli, and can with little difficulty be differentiated from true diphtheria bacilli by their appearance, mode of staining, and their cultural properties.

Differential Diagnosis.—The **method of staining suggested by Neisser,** as mentioned in the beginning of the chapter, is applicable especially to the recognition of the second form of pseudobacilli.

For the recognition of the non-toxin-producing form, **experiment on animals** is the only means of differentiating.

What appear to be **true diphtheria bacilli** have been found in the throat and mouth in about 1 per cent. of a number of **healthy persons** examined, but generally in individuals who have come into contact with diphtheria patients, or when diphtheria was prevalent in the community at the time of the examination. Those persons are always a source of danger to others, and they no doubt are in a great measure responsible for the spread of the disease.

The experiments of Roux and Yersin have shown that the various cultures of diphtheria bacilli have different potency in the production of toxins, and that occasionally bacilli grown under conditions, the same as much as possible, may at different times produce more or less toxins, and of a greater or lesser virulence. These facts bacteriologists are in no position to explain, and the toxicity of a diphtheria culture may only be determined by experimentation on animals.

The Antitoxin Treatment of Diphtheria.

The **discovery made by Roux,** that the diphtheria bacilli secrete a toxin which, when injected into susceptible animals, produces all the symptoms of true diphtheria, was soon followed by the **discovery of Behring**, which showed that the blood-serum of animals injected with the bacilli of diphtheria contains a substance which when inoculated into susceptible animals is able to immunize them from lethal doses of the bacilli.

These substances, called **antitoxins**, are obtained from animals having little or no susceptibility to the disease, and they have been used extensively both in the prevention and cure of diphtheria since 1894.

These **antitoxins** as exhibited therapeutically are obtained from the blood-serum of horses, as first suggested by Roux, and **are prepared** as follows:

Immunization.—A good-sized horse, which has been demonstrated to be *free from tuberculosis and glanders, by the injecting of tuberculin and mallein, and free from all rheumatic and chronic disease*, is gradually immunized to the diphtheritic poison by being injected with very small doses of the virulent toxins from a diphtheria bouillon culture filtrated through porcelain. The initial dose consists of 0.10 c.c. mixed with an equal quantity of Gram's iodine solution; this should produce little or no constitutional disturbance, and very little if any local effect. Four or five days after this first injection a second injection, consisting of pure toxin 0.10 c.c., is used, and every four or five days thereafter injections are repeated in progressively larger doses until the animal is able to withstand doses of from 400 to 500 c.c. of toxin. During those injections the animal may show decided local effects, such as swelling and œdema at the point of inoculation, but no very marked constitutional disturbances. During the progress of this immunization, at intervals, by puncturing of the jugular vein with a sterilized trocar, some blood is withdrawn from the animal and its serum tested as to its antitoxic value, and when the same is found sufficient the toxin injections are repeated at longer intervals to maintain the antitoxic property of the animal's serum, and the next process is begun.

Standardization.—A large quantity of blood, 4 or 5 liters, is extracted from the immunized horse at one time, collected in well-sterilized vessels, and allowed to clot in an ice-chest for two or three days, after which the clear serum is pipetted off and stored in sterilized flasks, the antiseptic strength of the serum being properly labelled on each flask. This antitoxin power, called **units**, is estimated as follows:

Ten times a fatal dose of a toxin, that is known to kill a 250-gram guinea-pig within three days, is mixed with different quantities of the serum to be tested, say, 0.10, 0.01, 0.001 c.c., and these mixtures injected into different guinea-pigs, Nos. 1, 2, and 3, respectively. Should guinea-pig No. 1 survive the mixed injection, and guinea-pigs Nos. 2 and 3 die, the antitoxin is said to contain 10 times 10 units in 1 c.c.; that is, it is an antitoxin of 100-unit power. Should guinea-pigs 1 and 2 survive, the antitoxin is one which in 1 c.c. has protecting powers amounting to 10 multiplied by 20, or 200 antitoxin units. Should guinea-pig No 3 also survive this injection, then the serum used is equivalent to 10 times 100, or 1000 antitoxin units per c.c.

No serum should be accepted for use in the treatment of diphtheria unless its immunizing or antitoxic power is equivalent to at least 200 units per c.c.; a serum used as a protective only may be accepted with 100 units antitoxic power per c.c.

In order to test the antitoxin and for the purpose of immunizing animals, it is necessary to produce toxins of a standard virulence. This, as has been seen, is not always a task of easy performance. The standard of toxins accepted in all laboratories and establishments in which antitoxin is manufactured is a toxin of which 0.10 c.c. is able to kill a 250- or 300-gram guinea-pig within three days, and no toxins should be used excepting such as have this power. It is best manufactured by growing virulent cultures of *Bacillus diphtheriæ* in large Erlenmeyer flasks, with free access of air and at a temperature of 37° C. The height of the toxicity of the culture is reached in about eight to ten days, when the culture should be removed from the incubator and filtered through a Chamberlain porcelain filter, tested on guinea-pigs, and if found of the required strength put away in sterile bottles. Unless it shows that 0.10 c.c. when injected into a guinea-pig of 250 grams causes death of the animal within three days, it should not be accepted.

The German government adopted this as a standard strength for toxins, and no antitoxin is put on the market unless its value has been tested by means of its power of neutralizing so many units of this standard toxin.

Value of the Antitoxin Treatment of Diphtheria.—It has now been used eight years; and has been of inestimable importance. As a **therapeutic agent** given within the first three days of the disease, it has reduced the mortality of diphtheria more than one-half. When used after the third day it is of less value, but still shows decidedly good effects.

When used as a **preventative** in persons exposed to the danger of contagion with this disease, it gives protection for several weeks.

Dose of Antitoxic Serum.—As a **prophylactic** from 200 to 500 units should be used, according to the age. For the purpose of **treatment** not less than 2000 to 3000 units should be injected at one time, and that as early as possible in the course of the disease; and this dose should be repeated in twenty-four hours unless decided beneficial effects are noticed.

The experience of the author, based on the examination of several thousand cases of diphtheria treated by serum in New Orleans, has shown that, with the exception of an occasional urticarial rash, no untoward effect follows this treatment. The explanation of this eruption has not been given, but it is very probably due to some other elements contained in the blood-serum of the horse, and appears to be much more common following the use of serum taken from some horses than from that of others; it appears to have no relation to the antitoxic power of the serum.

QUESTIONS.

When and by whom was the *Bacillus diphtheriæ* discovered?

How does it answer the postulates of Koch with regard to pathogenic bacteria?

Where is the *Bacillus diphtheriæ* found?

Describe the appearance of the Klebs-Loeffler bacillus.

Describe the staining of this bacteria.
What characterizes cultures of the diphtheria bacillus?
How are false or pseudobacilli differentiated from true diphtheria bacilli?
Describe the Neisser method of staining the diphtheria bacilli.
How does it behave in the presence of oxygen?
Is it motile?
Has it flagella?
Does it contain spores?
At what temperature does it grow?
What is its thermal death-point?
How does it behave in the presence of disinfectants?
How is it affected by direct sunlight?
How does it behave in the albuminous fluid? How in the dark?
How is Loeffler's blood-serum for the culture of the *Bacillus diphtheriæ* prepared?
Describe the growth of this bacillus on Loeffler's medium, in bouillon, on gelatin, on agar, on potato, in milk?
Why is diphtheria a toxic disease?
How is the toxin of diphtheria obtained?
Give the effects of inoculation of diphtheria bacilli on guinea-pigs.
What is the effect of the inoculation of those bacteria on mucous surfaces of animals?
How do the different cultures of *Bacillus diphtheriæ* vary as to their virulence?
Give the boards' of health measures for diagnosing diphtheria by means of cultures.
How is the inoculation of cultures made in those cases?
What are the sources of error in this form of examination?
What two forms of pseudobacilli are found?
How are they recognized from true virulent bacilli?
How is the toxin prepared?
How is it gauged?
What is constant diphtheria toxin?
What is the result of the antitoxin treatment of diphtheria?
What is the result of its prophylactic use?
What dose should be given as a prophylactic?
What dose should be given in the treatment of diphtheria cases?

CHAPTER XV.

TETANUS, MALIGNANT ŒDEMA, AND SYMPTOMATIC ANTHRAX.

TETANUS.

Bacillus Tetani.

History.—*Bacillus tetani* was discovered by **Nicolaier** in 1884, and cultivated by **Kitasato** in 1889.

It is **found** *a.* in wounds in cases of tetanus, *b.* as a saprophyte in the soil, especially manured soil of gardens and stables, and *c.* in the intestinal secretions of animals.

Morphology.—The bacillus of tetanus as obtained in cultures is seen in one of two forms, either in the **vegetative form** or as a **spore-bearing bacterium.**

Its **vegetative form** is a short rod with round ends, occurring singly or in pairs, or sometimes forming long filaments.

FIG. 60.

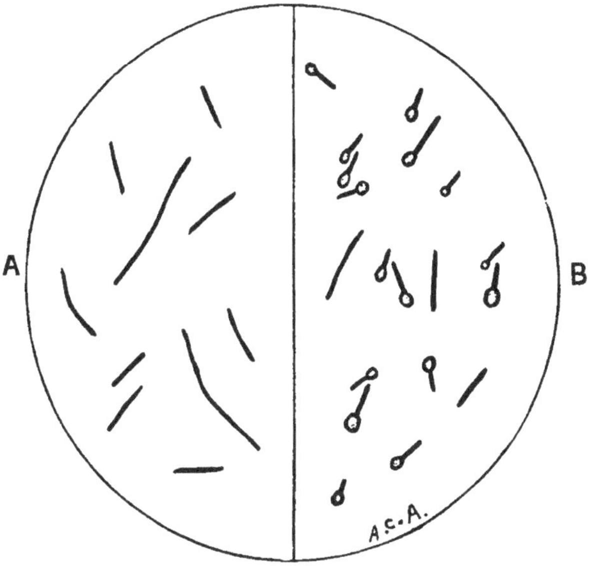

Bacillus tetani: A, vegetative stage; B, spore-stage, showing pin-shapes. (Abbott.)

Its **spore-bearing form** is quite characteristic, resembling a pin; this is due to the fact that the spore is formed at one end of the bacillus, and as the bacillus bulges at that portion the typical appearance of a pin is given to the bacillus (Fig. 60).

The *Bacillus tetani* **stains** with all the anilin dyes, and also by Gram's method.

Biologic Characters.—The *Bacillus tetani* is purely **anaërobic,** not developing at all in the presence of oxygen. It grows in all culture-media at a temperature as low as 18° or

20° C., but best at 37° C. It does not grow at a temperature below 14° C. Cultures must be kept in a **hydrogen atmosphere,** as the presence of the oxygen of the air prevents their growth.

On the surface of **gelatin** the cultures resemble very much those of the *Bacillus subtilis,* but liquefy the medium more slowly (Fig. 61).

In **gelatin stab-cultures** it grows in the depth of the medium, and the colonies have very much the appearance of a fir tree. Its growth is very slow in this medium, but the addition of from 1 to 2 per cent. of glucose to the gelatin increases materially the rapidity of the growth. The growth on **agar** is very much like that on gelatin, but it causes no liquefaction of the medium.

In **bouillon** it grows at 37° C., in the depth of the tube, with the production of gases. It does not cause coagulation of **milk,** and produces no acids in its cultures. **All cultures** of it are noted for their characteristic disagreeable odor.

To obtain pure cultures of the *Bacillus tetani,* a number of methods have been resorted to; that recommended by **Kitasato** is as follows:

The pus or secretion of the wound in a case of tetanus, or some garden or stable soil containing the sporing form of *Bacillus tetani,* is plated on agar, or streak cultures are made on this medium with the secretions of the wound or with the contaminated soil. These agar plates or tubes are kept at the temperature of the incubator for three or four days, so as to allow the growth of all bacteria contained therein. At

Fig. 61.

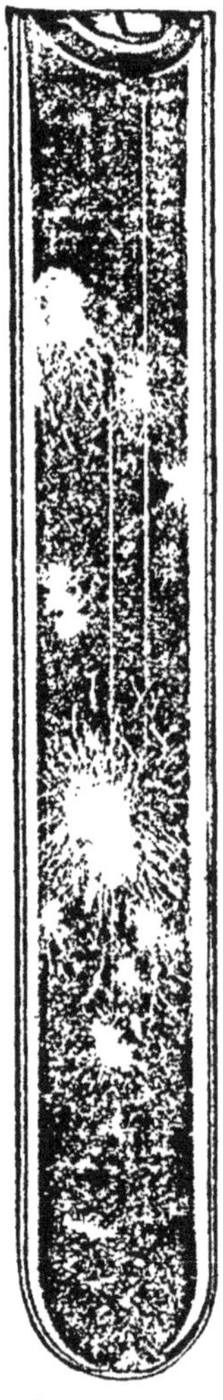

Colonies of the tetanus bacillus four days old, made by distributing the organisms through a tube nearly filled with glucose-gelatin. Cultivation in an atmosphere of hydrogen. (From Fraenkel and Pfeiffer.)

the end of that time cover-glass preparations are made from the colonies along the streak or on the surface of the agar plates. If some of the characteristic pin-shaped *Bacillus tetani* are found, the cultures are treated as follows: They are exposed from three-fourths to one hour to the temperature of 80° C.; in this way all the fully formed bacteria and the greater part of the spores are killed, the vegetative form of the *Bacillus tetani* included, but spores of this bacillus remain alive. Then from these cultures fresh gelatin, bouillon, or agar tubes are inoculated, and the same grown at the temperature of the room or incubator in an atmosphere of hydrogen. If the original substance experimented with contained the *Bacillus tetani*, characteristic cultures will be seen in this medium in a few days, and may subsequently be transplanted.

Motility and Thermal Death-Points.—The *Bacillus tetani* in the **spore-bearing variety** is non-motile; the **vegetative form** is quite motile, though no flagella have been discovered. A temperature of 58° C. will destroy the non-spore-bearing variety in a half-hour; 60° C. will kill them in five minutes; and 65° C. instantaneously. **Spores**, however, are able to resist a temperature of 80° C. for two hours, but are killed by a temperature of 100° C. in from four to five minutes. When dried, the spores are capable of retaining their vitality for months and years. Carbolic acid (5 per cent.) will not kill them in less than ten hours; but if 0.5 per cent. hydrochloric acid be added to the carbolic acid solution, spores will be destroyed in two hours. Bichloride of mercury (1 in 1000) will destroy them in three hours. Bichloride (1 in 1000) to which 0.5 per cent. hydrochloric acid has been added will kill them in thirty minutes.

Tetanin.—The *Bacillus tetani* secretes a powerful poison, known as tetanin, which diffuses in the cultures and is not retained in the cell-body.

The symptoms of tetanus are due to the action of this toxin, and not to the influence of the bacteria themselves. Tetanus is strictly a toxæmic disease. This is proved by the fact that inoculations with cultures of bacilli in which the toxins have been destroyed produce no symptoms whatever. These toxins are destroyed by a temperature of 60° to 65° C., by prolonged exposure to diffuse daylight, or by exposure for one hour to direct sunlight, and cultures containing spores so exposed are innocuous to animals.

The author has succeeded in several instances in obtaining the tetanus bacillus by the following **cultivation-method**:

After thoroughly heating a bouillon tube or a liquid gelatin tube so as to expel as much as possible all the oxygen, the culture is allowed to cool to a temperature a little below 80° C. The suspected material is then inoculated deep into the tube, and the surface of the medium is covered by a layer of 1 to 2 c.c. of paraffin oil, a cotton plug inserted, and a rubber cap applied over the tube.

In this way he has obtained cultures with great facility. In one case, notably, cultures were made from the surface of a nail, that caused a wound which produced tetanus in an adult. In another case a piece of diphtheritic membrane wrapped in a piece of gauze and kept on the hearth over night, was handed to him from a diphtheria patient for examination. The next day to his surprise besides the diphtheria bacilli a few bacilli resembling the tetanus bacilli were found. A piece of this membrane was inoculated into bouillon prepared in the foregoing manner, and he obtained after three or four days a pure culture of the tetanus bacillus which proved fatal to guinea-pigs.

Pathogenesis.—The animals susceptible to the *Bacillus tetani* are man, horses, guinea-pigs, rabbits, and mice. Dogs are little susceptible, and birds scarcely at all. Amphibians can not be infected. The **inoculation of animals** is made by means of a liquid culture **injected subcutaneously** or by means of some of the contaminated material introduced into a deep pocket in the subcutaneous tissue. The **period of incubation** is more or less prolonged, varying from a few days to occasionally two or three weeks. During this time the bacilli seem to be generating their poison. After this has been accomplished, the toxic effects are very marked and rapidly fatal, the symptoms showing first in the parts nearest to the point of inoculation. These **symptoms** consist in spasms of the muscular system, and generally end in death. The blood and the urine of inoculated animals is toxic to other susceptible animals.

At the **autopsy**, apart from the slight inflammatory changes at the point of inoculation, with occasionally the discovery of a few bacilli at that point, no changes are observed in the organs, excepting an intense congestion of the nervous system.

Bacilli deprived of toxins injected into animals are taken up by the phagocytes.

Preparation of the tetanus toxin is very easy. A bouillon culture of the *Bacillus tetani* is grown in an atmosphere of hydrogen at a temperature of 37° C. for from two to four weeks. At the end of that time the culture is filtered through a porcelain filter, and the filtrate is found to contain the tetanin, which is best kept in the dark, and preserved by the addition of 0.5 per cent. of phenol. The power of this toxin, called **tetanin**, is very great, $\frac{1}{5,000,000}$ c.c. being sufficient to kill a 15-gram mouse in three to four days. Occasionally this toxicity is very much increased, and Burger and Cohn have succeeded in obtaining tetanin, which in doses of $\frac{1}{50,000,000}$ c.c. was fatal to mice. This is by far the **most powerful poison known**; taken in this proportion it would mean that about $\frac{1}{5}$ milligram would be fatal to man. Compare this with atropine, the fatal dose of which is about 130 milligrams, and anhydrous prussic acid, the fatal dose of which is 54 milligrams, and a fair idea of its toxicity will be obtained.

Tetanin acts on animals only when introduced into the circulation; given by the mouth it possesses no poisonous properties.

The blood of animals dead or affected with tetanus is poisonous to other animals in the same way as cultures of the bacillus itself. But it is possible to inoculate animals with doses small enough to produce no fatal effects; and animals so inoculated are protected from future infection, and their blood and fluid secretions will serve to protect other animals when injected in doses less than the fatal dose. The discovery of this fact by Behring and Kitasato has been the opening wedge to serum therapy.

Tetanus antitoxin, like diphtheria antitoxin, is produced by inoculating large animals, like the horse, with minute doses of the toxin, diluted at first with Gram's iodine solution, and artificially establishing in the horse an immunity against the poison. The dose of the toxin is gradually increased, and injected every few days into the animals until immense doses (600 to 700 c.c.) may be injected at one time without producing any marked symptoms. When immunity has thus been secured, blood is taken from the animal and its serum tested, when it is found to have decided powers of neutralizing the toxin.

Tetanus antitoxin **is useful** chiefly as a **preventative** against tetanus, and in veterinary medicine has been found of great value. When applied to the human subject, however, the results have not been so satisfactory, for it is used then only as a therapeutic agent. At the time of its employment the symptoms of tetanus have generally shown themselves, and these are exceedingly rapid and violent in their effects, and commonly fatal. A number of observers have derived very decided benefit from its use, however, especially by injecting it into the ventricles of the brain, where it may act by directly and locally combating the poisonous action of the tetanin present.

Tetanus antitoxin **is measured** somewhat differently than is diphtheria antitoxin. Its strength is expressed as follows: 1 in 1,000,000 or 1 in 10,000,000. This means that 1 c.c. of the antitoxin is capable of protecting from infection 1,000,000 or 10,000,000 grams of guinea-pig. In some cases an antitoxin of 800,000,000-gram power has been obtained.

This antitoxin, however, does not retain its power very long, and **deteriorates quickly** in the fluid form. It is generally made into a powder, which may be dissolved into a neutral saline solution for use.

MALIGNANT ŒDEMA.

The Bacillus of Malignant Œdema.

History.—Malignant œdema is **caused** by a very malignant bacillus, **discovered** by **Pasteur, studied** by **Koch** and **Kitt**, and **found** in the soil of gardens and in the dust of streets, which, when inoculated into animals, rapidly produces the disease.

Morphology.—Rods from 3 to 5 mikrons in length and 1.10 mikron in thickness. They occur singly or in pairs in cultures, rarely forming threads. The ends are square in apposition when two bacilli come together, but rounded when the bacilli are single or at the free ends of united bacilli.

This bacillus **stains** with all the ordinary methods of staining, but does not stain by Gram's method.

It **forms spores**, situated at or near the centre of the bacillus, causing a swelling of the bacterium. (Plate III.)

Biologic Characters.—The bacillus of malignant œdema is an **obligate anaërobic**, and does not grow at all in the presence of oxygen. It grows in all culture-media in hydrogen gas, liquefies gelatin, and rapidly liquefies blood-serum.

In **gelatin** and **bouillon** it grows at the bottom of the tube, and in the liquid gelatin the colonies are in the form of spheres, which are scarcely discernible at first, but which, on account of the fermentation developed by the bacilli causing clouding of the medium, become more and more apparent.

On **agar plates** in a hydrogen atmosphere it grows as whitish bodies, which under the magnifying glass are seen to consist of branching and interlacing lines radiating irregularly from the centre to the periphery.

The colonies grow at ordinary temperature, but best at 37° C.

Pathogenesis.—Men, horses, calves, dogs, sheep, chickens, pigeons, rabbits, guinea-pigs, are all susceptible to the disease.

Inoculation of animals is performed **subcutaneously** by introducing a small particle of the suspected material or culture into a deep pocket. The **symptoms** developed in animals are a rapid and extensive œdema, with bloody effusions at the

PLATE III.

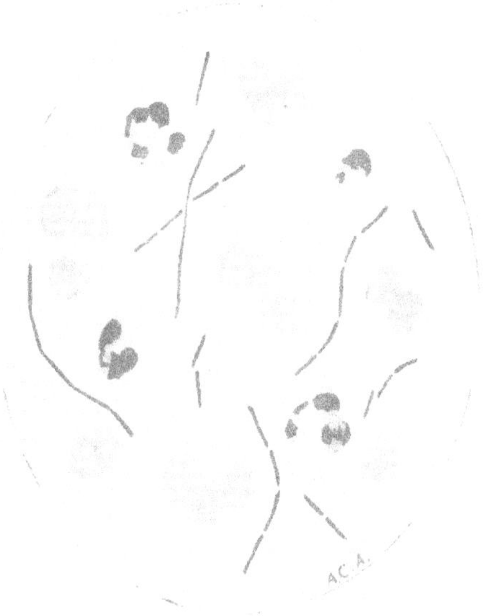

A

B

Bacillus Œdematis Maligni. (Abbott.)

A. Œdema-fluid, from site of inoculation of guinea-pig, showing long and short threads. B. Spore-formation, from culture.

point of inoculation, involving also the muscular tissues. The internal organs show little change, excepting the spleen, which is enlarged. The bacilli are rarely found in the blood of the heart when the **autopsy** is performed immediately after death, but they are found in limited numbers in the internal viscera. If the autopsy is delayed, however, the whole body of the animal becomes infected with the bacillus.

This bacillus is grown, like the tetanus and other anaërobics, in atmospheres of hydrogen only.

SYMPTOMATIC ANTHRAX.

Bacillus Anthracis Symptomatici.

History.—**Ferrer** and **Bollinger discovered** a bacillus in the disease of animals known as **black leg, quarter evil,** or **quarter ill,** which is also **found** in humid soils in certain localities during the summer months, especially when those places have been contaminated with discharges from infected animals.

Morphology.—The description of this microörganism given by Kitasato is as follows:

Actively motile rods, 3 to 5 mikrons in length, and from 0.5 to 0.6 mikron in thickness, occurring singly, occasionally in pairs, never forming filaments (Fig. 62).

It **stains** by all the anilin colors and by Gram's method. It **forms spores,** which are situated at or near one of the poles, giving a swollen appearance to the bacillus.

Biologic Characters.—In the **vegetative type** it is actively motile, but loses its motion in the **spore-bearing form.** It can not be cultivated in an atmosphere of oxygen. It is **purely anaërobic,** and does not grow in an atmosphere of carbonic acid gas.

It grows best when **glucose** (1.5 to 2 per cent.) or **glycerin** (4 to 5 per cent.) is added to the culture-medium. It grows in all media. It liquefies gelatin. It grows best at the temperature of the incubator, 37° C., but does not grow at a temperature below 14° C. In deep-seated punctures of **gelatin** or **agar** it grows in three or four days, and produces during its growth gas bubbles. The colonies appear as globules which cause liquefaction of the gelatin and coalesce into irregular lobulated liquid areas. The **dried spores** retain their vitality for months. They resist a temperature of 80° C. for one hour, but five minutes' exposure at 100° C. is sufficient to destroy them. Carbolic acid (5 per cent.) is not effective as a disinfectant in less than ten hours. The vegetative form, however, is killed in from three

FIG. 62.

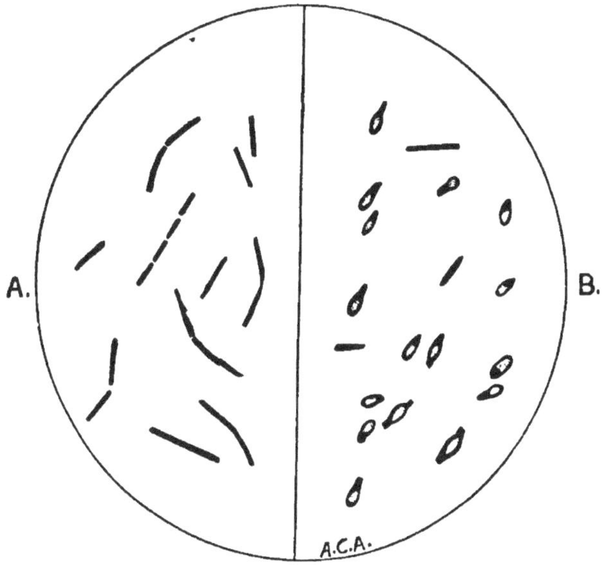

Bacillus of symptomatic anthrax: A, vegetative stage—gelatin culture; B, spore-forms—agar-agar culture. (Abbott.)

to five minutes. Bichloride of mercury (1 : 1000) will kill the spores in two hours.

Pathogenesis.—Cattle, sheep, goats, guinea-pigs, and mice are susceptible animals. Horses, asses, and rats show only slight local swelling, but no general infection. Dogs, cats, rabbits, chickens, pigeons, and hogs are immune. Inoculations are generally made deep into the subcutaneous tissue either with pure cultures of the microörganisms or from bits of tissue of a suspected animal. The **symptoms** are a rise of temperature, followed by painful swelling at the point of inoculation. Death takes place in from one to two days.

The **autopsy** reveals an extensive swelling of the subcutaneous tissues with emphysema. The œdematous fluid is blood-stained, and the muscles are dark and prominent. The lymphatic glands are involved. The internal organs show little change. In the fluid of the œdema the bacilli are found in large numbers, lying singly. Early autopsy reveals no bacteria in the blood, only a few in the internal organs. Late autopsy shows a considerable quantity of organisms that have invaded the whole body. The bacilli in the body are found to contain spores. This serves as a differentiation, in addition to other points, between it and the *Bacillus anthracis*.

Immunity.—One attack of the disease if not fatal affords protection against future attacks. The opposite of this happens with malignant œdema, one attack of which seems to predispose to other attacks.

QUESTIONS.

When, where, and by whom was the *Bacillus tetani* discovered and cultivated?

How many forms of the *Bacillus tetani* are there, and how are these distinguished?

What is the characteristic appearance of the spore-bearing form?

In what atmosphere does it grow best, and why?

What is the temperature-limit of its growth?

How does it grow in gelatin? In agar? In bouillon? In milk?

What is Kitasato's method of obtaining pure cultures of this bacillus?

In what form is it motile?

What agents and chemicals are the spores capable of resisting, and to what extent?

What is tetanin?

Describe a method of growing anaërobic bacilli with the use of paraffin oil.

What animals are susceptible to the infection of tetanus?

Describe the autopsy of an animal inoculated with *Bacillus tetani.*

Where and how are inoculations in animals made?

What symptoms are produced by tetanin injection?

What type of infection is tetanus?

How is tetanus toxin prepared?

What is the degree of toxicity of tetanin?

How is the antitoxin of tetanus prepared?

How is it used and for what purpose?

Why is it of more use in veterinary than in human medicine?

How is the strength of tetanus antitoxin expressed?

By whom was discovered the bacillus of malignant œdema?

Where is it found?

What is its appearance?

How does it stain?
How does it behave in the presence of oxygen?
How does it grow on different media?
What animals are susceptible?
How are inoculations performed?
What symptoms are produced by inoculation?
By whom was the bacillus of symptomatic anthrax discovered?
Where is it found?
What diseases of animals are produced by it?
Give the description of microörganisms containing spores and vegetative forms.
How does it stain?
What effect does the addition of glucose to media have upon the growth of this organism?
How does it grow in different media?
What are the effects of temperature on its growth?
How is it fatal to animals?
What animals are susceptible?
How is it differentiated from other bacilli?
What is the effect of a non-fatal attack of this disease?
How does symptomatic anthrax compare with malignant œdema?

CHAPTER XVI.

TYPHOID FEVER.

Bacillus Typhosus.

History.—The presence of a microörganism in cases of typhoid fever was **discovered by Eberth**, in 1880; it was named the *Bacillus typhosus;* but until **isolated and described by Gaffky**, in 1884, it was not fully recognized.

It is **found after death** in the blood, spleen, liver, intestines, Peyer's patches, and mesenteric ganglia, and **during life** in the blood, especially when the same is taken from the spleen by means of a hypodermatic syringe, in the rose patches, in the urine and feces, and **outside the human body**, occasionally in water and soil contaminated with dejecta of typhoid patients, and often in milk, which is due probably to the cleansing of the utensils in which the milk is collected with water contaminated with the bacilli (Figs. 63 and 64).

Morphology.—The *Bacillus typhosus* appears as a rod with rounded extremities, from 2 to 4 mikrons in length, and 0.6 to 0.8 mikron in breadth. At times it appears as short ovals; at others the bacilli are joined together, forming long threads. It **stains** with all the anilin dyes, but not quite so readily as other bacteria. It does not stain by Gram's method. In stained preparations clear spaces are observed in the body of the cells. This has given rise to the belief that the bacteria contain spores. There are, however, **no spores**, for those clear spaces do not stain by any of the spore-staining processes, and bacteria in which they are found are less resistant to external

FIG. 63.

Bacillus typhosus, from culture twenty-four hours old, on agar-agar. (Abbott.)

FIG. 64.

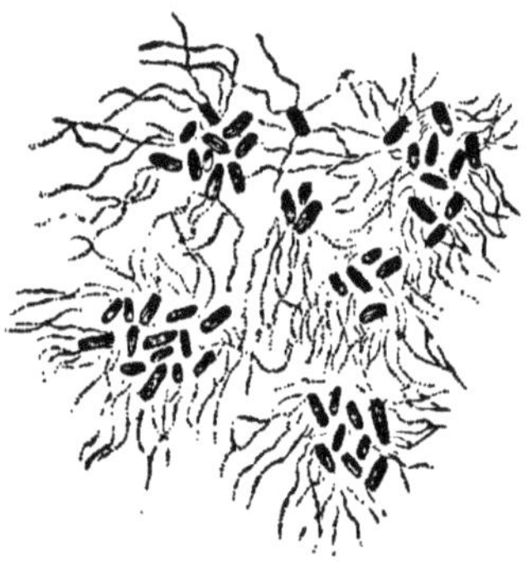

Bacillus typhosus, showing flagella stained by Loeffler's method. (Abbott.)

influences than others. This bacillus has numerous fine, hair-like **flagella**, which are not to be seen in unstained preparations or preparations stained by the ordinary methods, but it requires the flagella-stain of Loeffler to bring them out.

Biologic Characters.—The *Bacillus typhosus* is **aërobic**, but grows also without the presence of oxygen; it is therefore **facultative anaërobic.** It is non-spore-bearing, and is actively motile, the motions at times being very rapid. It grows in nearly all the artificial media, even at the room temperature, but best at a temperature of 37° C. Its growth at 20° C. is rather slow, but quite rapid at the temperature of the body.

On **gelatin plates** its colonies appear as small, yellowish, punctiform bodies, becoming in a short time round and irregularly notched, resembling droplets of oil. In **gelatin stab-cultures** they appear as small thick disks, finely dentated, of a pearl-like color. They do not liquefy gelatin.

On **agar plates** they appear as round, irregular, shiny colonies of a blue or grayish-white color, and develop very abundantly. In **agar stab-cultures** the growth is chiefly on the surface, and in the depth of the medium there is scarcely any appreciable development.

On **lactose-litmus agar** colonies are pale blue. On **potato** the growth is exceedingly variable, and not characteristic, as formerly believed. Sometimes it is scarcely appreciable, at other times it forms a film like a thin veil of the same color as the potato itself. Again, at times the growth is somewhat luxuriant and of a whitish color. It does not coagulate **milk.** It does not cause fermentation in **glucose-, lactose-, or saccharose-bouillon.** It does **not produce indol** in such quantity as is detected by the ordinary tests.

Vitality.—It is killed by an exposure of ten minutes to 60° C., and in much shorter time by exposure to higher temperatures. In the dried conditions it may be preserved for months.

Agglutination.—Persons who have suffered from an attack of typhoid fever or animals which have been inoculated with cultures of this bacillus have generated in their blood-serum a substance called **agglutinin.** This agglutinin has the property when mixed with cultures of the *Bacillus typhosus* of suddenly arresting the motion of the bacilli and of causing their **clumping** or **agglutination,** which is quite characteristic, and is made use of for the **diagnosis** of typhoid fever, as will be described later.

Pathogenesis.—None of the lower animals, as far as has been ascertained, is naturally susceptible to contract or develop typhoid fever. Indeed, the typical lesions of the disease as found in man have rarely been induced in the lower animals by inoculations with the typhoid bacillus.

Intraperitoneal, subcutaneous, and **intravascular inoculations,** in rabbits, guinea-pigs, and mice, will produce marked infection even in those animals, in the form of general septicæmia, in which the bacilli have been recovered in the general circulation and in the internal organs. The feeding of animals with articles contaminated with typhoid fever germs has in some instances, when the animal's vitality was very much lowered, produced infection, and sometimes lesions in the intestines and mesenteric ganglia very much resembling those found in human beings.

Differentiation of Bacillus Typhosus from Allied Groups.

I. General Features.—In many respects the *Bacillus typhosus* resembles very much the *Bacillus coli communis,* both from a morphological point of view as well as in its cultural peculiarities. The differentiation between the two is sometimes quite difficult, and it is necessary to cultivate the bacilli in all the known artificial media to come to a conclusion about their identity. The points of differentiation are the following:

The *Bacillus coli communis* is generally thicker and much less motile than the typhoid bacillus. The coli communis grows much more rapidly in all media. The flagella of the typhoid bacillus are more numerous. The *Bacillus typhosus* does not coagulate milk, and the coli communis does. Its growth on litmus-agar remains blue, that of the coli communis becomes red from the production of acids. The *Bacillus typhosus* produces no indol, as ascertained by the ordinary Dunham's test, but the coli communis produces indol very rapidly. The *Bacillus typhosus* does not produce fermentation in lactose or glucose media, whereas the coli communis produces fermentation and fermentative gases. On potato the growth of *Bacillus typhosus* is almost invisible, while that of *Bacillus coli communis* is abundant, creamy, and of a dark-brown color. The serum of the blood from typhoid fever cases agglutinates cultures of *Bacillus typhosus.* It has no action on *Bacillus coli communis*

II. Widal's and Chantemesse's Differentiation.—Two tubes of agar or gelatin to which 2 per cent. of lactose-sugar has been added are allowed to melt and a sufficient quantity of neutral litmus tincture is added to them to give a deep-violet color. The tubes are sterilized and are inoculated, one with the *Bacillus typhosus*, and the other with the *Bacillus coli communis*. If agar tubes are used, they are placed in the incubator at 37° C. When the colonies grow, those of the *Bacillus typhosus* retain the blue color, while the colonies of the *Bacillus coli communis* become of a bright-red color, and at the bottom of the tube can be seen bubbles of gas.

III. Elsner's Method of Differentiation.—This consists in employing an acid mixture of gelatin, potato juice, and potassium iodide, which contains neither peptone nor sodium chloride. It is used to separate not only the coli communis, but also the ordinary saprophytes from the *Bacillus typhosus*. The saprophytes do not develop at all in this medium, and the colonies of coli communis and *Bacillus typhosus* show marked differences in their behavior on plates made of this mixture, and are easily separated. At the end of twenty-four hours tubes of this mixture inoculated with the suspected material will contain a large number of coli communis colonies, which have the same appearance as cultures of this bacillus on ordinary agar plates, whereas there will scarcely be visible development of colonies of the *Bacillus typhosus*. After forty-eight hours the *Bacillus typhosus* will appear as small, pale, almost transparent colonies, easily distinguished from the dark granular colonies of the coli bacillus. According to Abbott, **Elsner's medium** is thus **prepared**:

"Grate 1 kilogram of pealed potato and allow this to stand over night in a refrigerator; then press out all juice, using an ordinary meat-press for the purpose; filter this fresh juice cold to remove as much of the starch-granules as possible. *If this is not done, the starch when heated swells to such an extent as to render filtration almost impracticable.* Boil the filtrate and again filter. Test the filtrate for acidity by titrating 10 c.c. with a decinormal solution of sodium hydroxide, the indicator used being 6 drops of the ordinary 0.5 per cent. solution of phenolphtalein in 50 per cent. alcohol. The acidity of the juice should be such as to require 3 c.c. of a decinormal sodium hydroxide solution to neutralize 10 c.c. of the juice. If the acidity is found to be greater than this, which is usually the case, dilute with water until the proper degree is reached. If less than this, the juice may be concentrated by evaporation. It is desirable that this acidity should be due to the acids normally present in the potato, and that it should not be artificially obtained by the addition of other acids. Now add 10 per cent. of gelatin (with no peptone and no sodium chloride present), dissolve by boiling, and again test the acidity, using 10 c.c. of the mixture and phenolphtalein as before. Deduct 3 c.c. (the acidity of the potato juice that is to be maintained) from the number of c.c. of the decinormal sodium hydroxide solution requisite to neutralize the 10 c.c. of the gelatin mixture, and from the resulting figure calculate the amount of normal solution of sodium hydroxide needed for the entire volume, and add it. Boil, clarify with an egg, and filter through paper in the usual manner. To the filtrate add potassium iodide in the proportion of 1 per cent., decant into tubes, and sterilize."

IV. Stodard's and Hiss' Differentiation.—By this method use is made of the great motility of the *Bacillus typhosus* to differentiate it from the coli communis. It is valuable at times. Success in this procedure depends on the important fact that in a semifluid mixture the *Bacillus typhosus*, on account of its great motility, will diffuse much more rapidly from the point of inoculation to nearly all parts of the medium, whereas the coli communis, having only a sluggish or no motion at all, develops only at the place of immediate inoculation. For detailed accounts of these methods the reader is referred to larger treatises on bacteriology.

Sources of Pure Cultures.—From the spleen of typhoid fever cases pure cultures of the bacillus may be readily obtained, in early autopsies, and during life; blood extracted by means of a hypodermatic syringe from this organ will almost always show the bacillus. Indiscriminate punctures of the spleen during life, however, are not to be recommended, as this procedure is not free from danger.

The *Bacillus typhosus* has occasionally been obtained from abscesses in the subcutaneous tissue and internal organs in pure cultures in some cases of typhoid fever, showing that this bacillus is at times the cause of suppuration.

Artificial Susceptibility.—Animals resisting the effects of inoculation with the *Bacillus typhosus* can be made susceptible by the simultaneous introduction of other saprophytes which seem to overcome their immunity.

The Blood-Serum Diagnosis of Typhoid Fever.

The diagnosis of typhoid fever by the blood-serum method is to-day generally employed. As mentioned before, this is **based on the principle discovered by Pfeiffer,** that the blood of persons suffering with typhoid fever, or who may recently have had the disease, when mixed with young cultures of Eberth's bacillus, has the property of arresting the active motion of the bacilli, and causing their agglutination or clumping. This power resides in the serum, and is due to a substance called **agglutinin.**

Widal inaugurated the blood-test for typhoid fever, and suggests that to 1 c.c. of bouillon culture, not more than twenty-four hours old, and grown at a temperature of 35° C., 0.10 c.c. of the serum to be tested be added. The serum may be obtained either by allowing the drawn blood to coagulate, or by means of a small blister. In the space of from five to ten minutes all motion of the bacilli is arrested, and these come together, forming peculiar clumps. This clumping may be seen both in the hanging drop, and even by the naked eye in culture-tubes. Ordinarily the hanging-drop method is adopted, as it requires much less serum, and is therefore less injurious and vexatious to the patient.

Wyatt Johnston's Dried Blood Method.—This observer has demonstrated that the same reaction may be obtained by the use of dried blood instead of fresh serum, and that even after the blood has been dried for several days or weeks it still retains its agglutinating power. The **procedure in detail** is as follows:

A drop of the blood to be tested is obtained from the finger or lobe of the ear and allowed to dry on a clean slide. With a platinum wire a few loopfuls of sterile water are mixed with the dried blood and the same is diluted until about of the same color as normal blood. One loopful of this blood mixture is added to 40 or 50 loopfuls of a bouillon culture of the *Bacillus typhosus* twenty hours old, on a cover-glass, and a hanging drop made in the usual way. In the course of a half- to one hour, if the blood comes from a case of typhoid fever of sufficient duration, not less than six or seven days, cessation of motion and clumping of the bacteria in the culture drop will have been completely effected.

In the experience of the author in the Municipal Laboratory of New Orleans with more than 6000 cases, this test

FIG. 65.

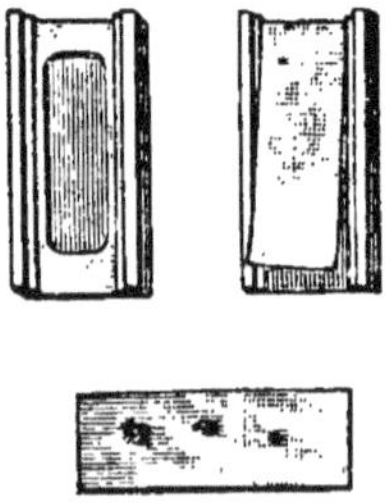

Outfit used by the Municipal Laboratory of New Orleans for the collection of blood for the typhoid fever test.

has given satisfactory results. The plan, which is a **modification of the New York Board of Health method.** is as follows:

At the diphtheria depots blood slides are left with blank forms giving directions (Fig. 65).

Directions for Preparing Specimen of Blood.—Clean thoroughly the tip of the finger or lobe of the ear, and prick with a clean needle deep enough to cause several drops of blood to exude; two or three drops are then placed on the slide of the outfit. Let the blood dry, then place the slide in holder, fill out the blank form, and return to depot where obtained. On the following day a report of the result of examination will be mailed or telephoned to the attending physician.

The blood only of fever patients is to be used. Should the report be negatived and the case be suspicious, the physician in attendance is requested to send another specimen, and in every case to notify the bacteriologist as to whether the laboratory diagnosis is finally in harmony with the clinical diagnosis or at variance with it.

Sources of Error.—One, which must be remembered, is due in some cases to the persistence of the reaction for a number of years after a typhoid attack : so that a reaction may appear in health or in affections other than typhoid fever, if the patient has previously suffered from the disease. In cases in which the reaction is marked, it may apparently be positively stated that the patient has, or has had, typhoid fever within a few years.

Diagnostic Values.—If the reaction is present, but not well marked, only probable diagnosis may be made. If the reaction is absent in a patient sick seven days, the diagnosis of typhoid fever may be excluded.

The experiment has not been tried long enough and not in a sufficient number of cases to permit a positive statement as to the earliest date of the appearance of the reaction in typhoid fever.

Vaccination Against Typhoid Fever.

Wright and **Semple** have recently practised the vaccination of human beings against typhoid fever, and extensive observations have been made in India and South Africa in the British Army. For this purpose a **typhoid vaccine** consisting of a bouillon emulsion made from a slant agar culture of the *Bacillus typhosus* twenty-four hours old is used. The culture is killed by heating it for five minutes at a temperature of 60° C. From a half to a quarter of the whole culture is used for one vaccination, and the culture must be of such a strength that a fourth of it is capable of killing a 300- to 400-gram guinea-pig, when the same is injected into it, without killing the bacilli.

The results obtained by these vaccinations have been encouraging and seem to open up a promising field for the serum-therapy of typhoid fever.

Antityphoid Serum.—Bokenham has recently succeeded in immunizing a horse by using a filtered bouillon culture of the typhoid bacillus, and he claims that the horse's serum has immunizing power when injected into guinea-pigs.

QUESTIONS.

What name is usually given to the microörganism causing typhoid fever?
By whom and when was it discovered?
Where is it found in the human body?
Where is it occasionally found outside of the human body?
Describe the *Bacillus typhosus.*
What are its staining peculiarities?
How do you stain the flagella of the *Bacillus typhosus?*
Why do you say that it contains no spores?
How does it behave in the presence of oxygen?
Is it motile?
At what temperature does it grow best?
What is its growth on gelatin? On agar? On lactose-litmus-agar? On potato? In Dunham's solution? In the fermentation-tube?
Does it liquefy gelatin?
What is the thermal death-point of the *Bacillus typhosus?*
What is agglutinin?
How are animals inoculated with the *Bacillus typhosus?*
What are the points of difference between the *Bacillus typhosus* and the *Bacillus coli communis?*
Give the Widal-Chantemesse method of distinguishing between colonies of typhoid and coli communis?
Give Elsner's method of separating the *Bacillus typhosus* from the *Bacillus coli communis* and water bacteria.
Give Abbott's mode of preparing Elsner's medium.
On what are Stodard's and Hiss' methods based?
In what organ may the bacillus be obtained in pure cultures?
How may the resistance of animals to typhoid inoculation be overcome?
On what does the serum-test of typhoid fever depend?
How may serum be obtained for this test?
Describe the methods pursued with dried blood in municipal laboratories.

CHAPTER XVII.

Bacillus Coli Communis.

History.—It was **discovered** by **Escherich**, 1885, and **is found in health** as a constant inhabitant of the intestinal tract—chiefly in the large intestine—and also in the excretions from that tract. **In pathological conditions** it is met with, in association with other bacteria, *a.* In acute enteritis, cholera morbus, in certain forms of dysentery; it is easily demonstrable in large numbers, and has been thought by some to be the cause of those diseases, but this is not so. Its presence in the healthy individual in nearly all cases is sufficient to show the falsity of this position. *b.* It has also been found in cases of peritonitis, endocarditis, and in suppurating inflammation of the liver and the kidney. At **autopsies** it occurs in various organs and in nearly all conditions. Associated with specific microörganisms it has also been proved to exist in the blood of patients *in articulo mortis.* **Outside the human body** it has been discovered in water and soil contaminated with fecal matter.

Etiologic Relations.—For a long time this bacillus was looked upon as a harmless saprophyte; latterly experiments have established the fact that it is often the cause of inflammatory conditions in the body, and that in a number of other instances it is pathogenic from the fact that it lowers the vitality of the body and enables other germs to act deleteriously.

Morphology.—This bacillus is polymorphous and very closely resembles the typhoid bacillus in shape. It is a rod with rounded extremities, in very young cultures appearing almost oval with a bright centre. Later on the bacilli coalesce and appear as long threads. They possess flagella; not so numerous, however, as the *Bacillus typhosus.* These flagella may be stained by the Loeffler method. It has **no spores** and **stains** by all the ordinary anilin dyes, but not by the Gram method.

Biologic Characters.—It is **aërobic** and **facultative anaërobic.** It is motile at times, and at other times appears to be motionless. Its motility is always of the sluggish kind. Cultures which when young contain organisms with decided motion, have on being kept for some time shown that the bacilli have lost their motility. It grows on all the artificial culture-media and at the temperature between 10° and 40° C. Its growth, though retarded at the temperature above 40° C., is not altogether stopped until 45° C. is reached. Exposure to a temperature of 65° C. for five minutes destroys the bacteria. Exposure to cold has no effect on the bacteria, and in some instances the author has been able to cultivate bacteria which had been exposed to the temperature of liquefied air for several minutes.

In **bouillon** the bacillus grows very rapidly and renders the bouillon cloudy; pellicles are formed on the surface of the medium, and there is also a thick deposit at the bottom of the tube. A strong fecal odor can be detected.

On **gelatin plates** the colonies appear as small, spherical, blue-gray points, somewhat dentated at the margin. With a magnifying glass the colonies are brownish, lozenge-shaped or irregularly round, coarsely granular. In **gelatin stab-cultures** along the track of the needle are seen a series of small spherical colonies in rows and separated from each other. On the surface of the tube the growth is of a dirty gray color. It does not liquefy gelatin.

On **agar-agar** the growth has nothing characteristic. On **agar** to which 2 per cent. glucose has been added bubbles may be seen along the line of growth, due to the gases of fermentation. On **lactose-litmus-agar** the colonies develop very rapidly and are of a pinkish color. On **potato** it grows rapidly in the beginning, being of a bright-yellow color which later becomes brown. The growth in **serum** is similar to that on agar.

It produces indol in **peptone** solution and coagulates milk very rapidly. It ferments lactose- and glucose-bouillon.

Pathogenesis.—Bouillon cultures of this bacillus **injected intravenously** or **into the peritoneal cavity** of a rabbit cause death in less than twenty-four hours. On **autopsy** intense hyperæmia of the peritoneum, ecchymotic spots of the intestines, swelling of Peyer's patches, and enlargement of the spleen are found. **Subcutaneous inoculations** are followed by abscesses formed at the point of inoculation and by internal conditions similar to those produced by intravascular injections. Injected **into the pleural cavity** it gives rise in twenty-four hours to a purulent pleurisy accompanied by a large effusion in the cavity and the formation of false membrane.

QUESTIONS.

When and by whom was the *Bacillus coli communis* discovered?
Where is it found in the body in health? In pathological conditions?
What pathological conditions are found to be due to the presence of this microörganism?
Where is it found outside the human body?
Describe the *Bacillus coli communis.*
How do its flagella compare with those of the typhoid bacillus?
How is it stained?
How does it behave in reference to oxygen?
What is peculiar about its motility?
How does it grow on artificial media and at what temperature?
What is its thermal death-point?
What is the effect of cold?
How does it grow in bouillon? On gelatin? On lactose-litmus-agar? On potato? In milk? In Donovan's peptone solution?
What is the effect of intraperitoneal and intravascular inoculations in animals?
What lesions are found at the autopsy?
What lesions are produced by subcutaneous inoculation? By intrapleural inoculation?

CHAPTER XVIII.

ASIATIC CHOLERA.

Spirillum Choleræ Asiaticæ (Comma Bacillus).

History.—In the Cholera Congress at Berlin, 1884, **Koch** made the announcement that he had been able to isolate from the intestinal dejecta of cholera patients a microörganism which he believed to be the cause of the disease. His experiments were carried out in a number of cholera-infested places and on a large number of patients. His conclusions, though very much questioned at the time, are to-day accepted by all, and his *Spirillum choleræ Asiaticæ*, more commonly known as the comma bacillus, is recognized as the **etiological factor** in Asiatic cholera.

Morphology.—This microörganism belongs to the class of spirilla called by some authorities **vibrios.**

It **is found** in the secretions of cholera patients and in cultures as a short curved rod, from 0.8 to 2 mikrons in length, by 0.3 to 0.4 mikron in breadth. Sometimes two of these rods are united together by either end, with the convex surface looking different ways, appearing then as the Roman letter S; at other times a number of the rods are united together forming a long spirillum. These latter forms are especially seen in older cultures. In young cultures the rods are generally single or lying together and parallel to each other. *This peculiar mode of grouping serves in the recognition of this bacterium.*

The *Spirillum choleræ Asiaticæ* **stains** with all the anilin dyes, but rather poorly. It seems to have a more active

FIG. 66.

Spirillum of Asiatic cholera. Impression cover-slip from a colony thirty-four hours old. (Abbott.)

FIG. 67.

Involution-forms of the spirillum of Asiatic cholera, as seen in old cultures. (Abbott.)

affinity for the fuchsin dye. It does not stain by the Gram method. Young cultures take the stain much more readily than older cultures, and in these what is known as **involution-forms**—long, thready filaments of different thickness—are often found. The spirillum contains **no spores**, but has a single flagellum at each end (Figs. 66 and 67).

Biologic Characters.—The comma bacillus is strictly **aërobic**, and though it grows in an atmosphere in which the oxygen is diminished, it can not grow in the absence of this gas. This fact is the cause of its surface growth in fluid media.

It is an artificially motile spirillum, especially when lately obtained from cholera cases or in young cultures. It grows in all artificial media, provided these are neutral or slightly alkaline.

Its growth on **gelatin plates** and **stab-cultures** is quite characteristic. At the end of a few hours on gelatin plates the colony appears as a light whitish point, which grows very rapidly, liquefying slightly the gelatin around it. This

FIG. 68.

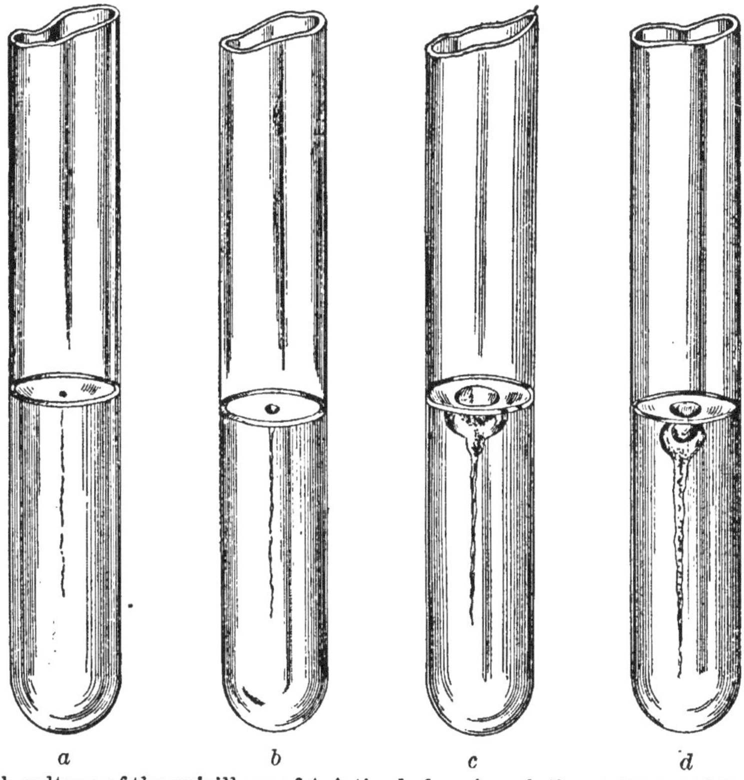

Stab-culture of the spirillum of Asiatic cholera in gelatin, at 18° to 20° C.: *a*, after twenty-four hours; *b*, after forty-eight hours; *c*, after seventy-two hours; *d*, after ninety-six hours. (Abbott.)

liquefaction of the gelatin seems to be accompanied by evaporation of the liquid, so that the colony sinks into the depth of the space left in the gelatin by the liquefaction, and the whole surface of the plate seems to be punched out. In **gelatin stab-cultures** the surface growth shows liquefaction of the gelatin around the colony, and this liquefaction gradually enlarges and extends along the track of the inoculating needle, being broader at the surface and forming a short funnel, which from the evaporation of the liquefied gelatin at the top gives it a characteristic appearance (Fig. 68).

Its growth on **agar** resembles very much the growth on gelatin, but the medium is not liquefied. **Milk** is coagulated by the formation of acids in the medium. In **peptone-bouillon** the medium is clouded, and a pellicle forms on the surface.

Vitality.—Its growth is very rapid, and advances best at a temperature between 35° and 37° C., but continues at a temperature as low as 17° C. Its growth is stopped at a temperature of 16° C., and the bacterium is destroyed in five minutes by an exposure to 65° C. Freezing does not destroy it. Dryness destroys it very rapidly, but in the moist state it may be kept frequently for several days and sometimes for several months.

Rapidity of Growth.—When associated with other bacteria in cultures it grows at first much more readily than any of the known bacteria, having a tendency to form a surface growth. At the end of eighteen to twenty hours, however, it is outstripped in its growth by the other bacteria, and in twenty-four to forty-eight hours its growth ceases altogether, and in a few days scarcely any spirillum may be found in the cultures. This is not due to the fact that it is destroyed by its association with the other bacteria, but more because the pabulum necessary for its growth is consumed. The rapidity of the growth of this bacterium and the fact of its growing on the surface of liquids are a great help in its isolation from cholera dejecta, which when diluted with a large amount of peptone-bouillon shows in a few hours a peculiar surface growth, which consists almost of a pure culture of cholera spirilla.

Pathogenesis.—None of the domestic animals contracts the disease naturally. But their immunity seems to be due to the fact that the bacteria that they ingest at the time that they are exposed are destroyed by the acidity of the gastric juice.

Artificial Susceptibility.—A number of ingenious devices have been resorted to to render animals susceptible to inoculation of the comma bacillus.

The **method of Koch** is ingenious and very successful. It consists in neutralizing the acidity of the gastric juice in a guinea-pig by the inoculation of 10 c.c. of a 5 per cent. solution of carbonate of sodium. This is introduced into the stomach by means of a soft catheter. A few minutes afterward 10 c.c. of young bouillon cultures of the cholera spirillum are introduced also **into the stomach** through the same catheter, and immediately an intraperitoneal injection of 1 c.c. of laudanum is made into the animal, for the purpose of retarding peristaltic action. The animal for an hour or so remains in a stupefied condition from the action of the opiate, but it soon revives. It shows, however, a complete loss of appetite, and at the end of twenty-four hours begins to show signs of paralysis of the hind extremities, with coldness of the surface. This paralysis gradually increases until in forty-eight hours the animal dies, showing pathologically some lesions resembling those found in man in cases of cholera—*i. e.*, a large amount of white serous exudate in the intestinal canal, with intense congestion of the intestines. Pure colonies of the spirillum may be obtained from these secretions.

Intraperitoneal injections in animals are followed by death in two or three hours. The symptoms are those of a rapid and intense peritonitis.

Immunity.—When the injections into animals are made in quantities too small to produce death the animal is protected for a time from subsequent fatal doses, and its serum has been found useful to protect animals of the same species against inoculations with fatal doses of the bacteria.

The blood-serum of these immunized animals, as well as that of cholera patients, has been found in a dilution of 1 to 50 to possess the power of **agglutination** when mixed with young bouillon cultures of the bacteria. This may be used as a **diagnostic test** of the disease.

The organism is seldom or never found in the general circulation nor in the internal organs of cholera cases.

Diagnosis.—For this purpose the rate of the growth on gelatin plates and the rapidity of the indol-formation in Dunham's solution are made use of. The experiments are carried on as follows:

The small flocculent masses found in the discharges of choleraic patients are taken and mixed with a large quantity of diluted peptone-bouillon, or preferably with Dunham's solution of peptone, and put into the incubator for three or four hours. At the end of that time a few drops from the surface of the liquid are taken and inoculated on gelatin plates, when characteristic colonies are developed in a few hours. Cover-glass preparations are also made, and if rods with a morphological appearance of cholera bacteria are found, agar plates are also made in this way. Melted agar is poured into Petri dishes, and these put into the incubator for a few hours in order to allow the evaporation water to collect on the surface of the agar; this water is poured off and the dishes inoculated by streaking the surface with the suspected material. In a very short time characteristic colonies develop along the line of the streak.

The cholera bacteria are of very rapid growth, but possess little or no resisting power, being destroyed by the physical measures just mentioned, and also in a very short time by the use of weak disinfectants.

Vaccinations against cholera have been performed on an extensive scale in cholera-infected countries. **Haffkine's method of injecting** attenuated or small doses of virulent cultures of the cholera spirillum as a means of protection against an attack of cholera seems to have rendered considerable service in protecting persons exposed to the disease; and experiments made by Ferran, in Spain, with attenuated cultures seem to have given encouraging results at the time of the cholera visitation.

QUESTIONS.

When and by whom was the *Spirillum choleræ Asiaticæ* (comma bacillus) discovered?

Describe the spirillum.

What is the peculiar arrangement of the bacteria in cultures and secretions?

How does the comma bacillus stain?
Does it contain spores?
Has it flagella?
How does it behave in the presence of oxygen?
Is it motile?
What condition of the media is necessary for its growth?
How does it grow on gelatin plates? In stab-cultures? On agar? In peptone-bouillon?
At what temperature does it grow?
What is its thermal death-point?
What is the effect of cold? Of dryness?
How long may it be kept in a moist state?
How does it grow when associated with other bacteria?
What peculiarities of its growth are made use of in those cases to isolate it?
What is the cause of the natural immunity of domestic animals to cholera?
How has Koch succeeded in inoculating the lower animals through the stomach?
What effect has inoculation of animals with cultures of the comma bacillus?
What is the effect of intraperitoneal inoculation?
How are animals made immune against cholera inoculation?
What is the effect of the blood-serum of immunized animals on other animals?
Where are the organisms found in cholera patients or at the autopsy in a cholera case?
How is the cholera bacillus isolated from cholera dejecta?
How much resisting power has the comma bacillus?
What is Haffkine's method of protection against cholera?

CHAPTER XIX.

INFLUENZA.

Bacillus of Influenza.

History.—In 1892 **Pfeiffer** and **Cannon** independently **isolated** from the bronchial and nasal secretions of cases of influenza, and from the blood in some cases, a small microorganism which they believed, with apparent correctness, to be the cause of the disease.

Morphology.—The bacillus so isolated may be described as follows: a small, thick rod, occurring singly or in pairs, **stained** with difficulty by the ordinary anilin dyes, but fairly well with a diluted Ziehl solution or Loeffler's methylene-blue; not stained by Gram's method. The body of the rod stains less well than the ends. It has no flagella and contains no spores. (Plate IV.)

PLATE IV.

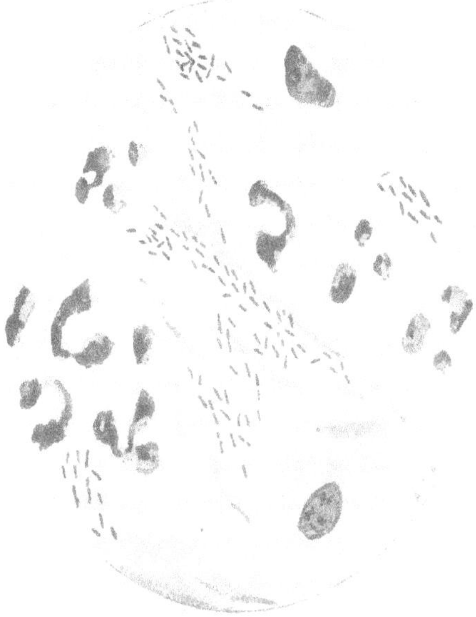

Bacillus of Influenza in Sputum. (Abbott.)

Biologic Characters.—The bacillus of influenza is strictly **aërobic,** not growing at all without oxygen. It is non-motile, and grows at a temperature between 26° and 43° C.

It grows but rather poorly in all media that may be submitted to this temperature, unless the surface of the media be smeared over with fresh sterilized blood, when the growth is quite luxuriant. On **glycerin-agar** or in **blood-serum** tubes on which fresh rabbit's blood has been smeared, it grows as transparent watery colonies, resembling very much dewdrops. The colonies have no tendency to coalesce. In **bouillon** to which a little fresh blood has been added it grows luxuriantly. It does not cause clouding of the medium, but its colonies are seen as little flakes adhering to the sides of the tube and forming a deposit at the bottom.

Vitality.—The bacillus of influenza is destroyed in two or three hours by drying. It has very little resisting power, and in water lives scarcely twenty-four hours. In pneumonia occurring during the course of this disease the bacilli are often found in the body of the leucocytes.

Pathogenesis.—Outside of the human race none of the lower animals seems to be susceptible to the disease, excepting perhaps the monkey, and by inoculation it is difficult to produce any symptom in laboratory animals. In man, however, the bacillus is constantly found in the bronchial and nasal secretions, also in the pneumonic patches so often found in the course of this disease. At **autopsies** it has been found also in the spleen and occasionally in the blood. Some persons have a natural power of retaining live bacilli in the lungs for a considerable length of time; especially is this the case with tuberculous patients, in whose sputum is very often found the *Bacillus influenzæ.* By **inoculating animals in the brain,** the nervous phenomena of this disease have been easily reproduced.

QUESTIONS.

By whom and when was the bacillus of influenza discovered?
Describe this bacillus and its staining peculiarities?
Does it possess flagella? Spores?
What are the principal biologic characters of the bacillus of influenza?

At what temperature does it grow?
In what artificial media does it grow?
What must be added to this media to facilitate its growth?
What is the appearance of the colonies, in glycerin? On agar? In blood-serum?
How does it grow in bouillon?
What is the resisting power of this bacillus?
What animals are susceptible?
Where is the bacillus found in animals?
What is peculiar about the retention of this bacillus by some persons?
How may this explain the spread of the disease?

CHAPTER XX.

BUBONIC PLAGUE.

Bacillus Pestis.

History.—Under various names and from the remotest times epidemics of bubonic plague have appeared in the old world, causing an immense fatality.

Yersin and **Kitasato**, in 1894, working independently, have both **discovered** the pathogenic germ of this disease in the suppurating buboes, blood, internal organs, and excretions of persons affected, and called it the *Bacillus pestis.*

Morphology.—This bacillus is a short, oval, thick rod, occurring singly or in pairs, or sometimes by the union of a number forming long filaments or threads. Staining with all the anilin dyes, but not by Gram's method. In stained preparations the centre of the bacilli cell stains less well than the ends of the rod, giving it quite a characteristic appearance. (Plate V.)

This bacillus has no flagella.

Biologic Characters.—The *Bacillus pestis* is a non-motile **aërobic.** It grows at all temperatures, but best between 36° and 39° C. It is killed by a temperature of 80° C. after an exposure of a half-hour, and in five minutes by an exposure to 100° C. in the steam sterilizer. It grows in all the arti-

PLATE V.

A

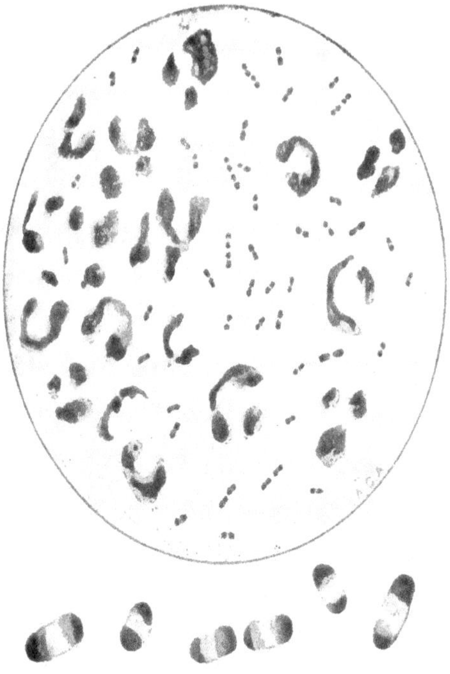

B

Bacillus of Bubonic Plague (Abbott.)

A. In pus from suppurating bubo. *B*. The bacillus very much enlarged to show peculiar polar staining.

ficial media. On **gelatin**, after twenty-four or thirty-six hours the colonies appear as small, sharply defined, round, white masses which do not liquefy the medium. Its growth in **agar** in the incubator is a little more rapid than in gelatin. It does not cloud **bouillon.** Cultures in this medium show a number of flocculi in the tube and a deposit at the bottom. It does **not cause fermentation,** and it gives **no indol reaction.** It coagulates **milk.**

Vitality.—The *Bacillus pestis* is very susceptible to the action of disinfectants, 1 per cent. carbolic acid being sufficient to kill it in one hour.

Pathogenesis.—Man, mice, rats, guinea-pigs, rabbits, cats, hogs, horses, chickens, and sparrows are very susceptible to the disease. Pigeons, dogs, amphibia, and bovines appear to enjoy immunity. *During an epidemic of bubonic plague susceptible animals seem to contract the disease naturally.*

For experimentation **subcutaneous inoculation** with liquid cultures of the bacillus is generally resorted to. The **changes produced** are: Swelling of œdematous character at the point of inoculation, and involvement of the lymphatic glands; death resulting in from twenty-four to forty-eight hours. At the **autopsy** the local swelling is found to be due to an œdematous condition of the part, the bloody fluid containing a large number of bacilli. The neighboring lymphatic glands are also greatly inflamed, and some of them are found suppurating. In their substance the pest bacilli are also found in great number. There also occurs a purulent exudate in the peritoneal and pleural cavities. The internal organs, liver, lungs, adrenal bodies, and spleen are very much affected.

Three forms of the disease are recognized in man: the **bubonic or ganglionic,** the **septicæmic,** and the **pneumonic** form, the most frequent of these being the bubonic, and the most fatal the pneumonic.

Infection generally takes place through an abrasion of the skin, but the disease may be caused by inhalation of the pest bacilli.

The usual form of the disease presents the following **symptoms**: a sudden rise of temperature accompanied by great prostration and delirium, and the occurrence of lymphatic swellings (buboes) affecting chiefly the glands corresponding to the inoculated portion. These become very much enlarged, and have a tendency to soften and suppurate. In severe cases death occurs in forty-eight hours; in others, the duration of the disease is somewhat longer. The **prognosis** is more favorable, the longer the duration of the disease. Characteristic bacilli are found in the lymphatic glands, and also occasionally in the blood.

Immunity.—Persons who have recovered from an attack of bubonic plague or animals that have survived inoculations are found to be immune for a certain period of time. This immunity is due to a substance developed in the serum of those animals, which may also when inoculated into susceptible animals protect them from infection with bubonic plague. **Artificial immunity** may also be conferred by injecting cultures of the dead bacilli.

Agglutination.—The serum of immune animals possesses also an agglutinating action when mixed with bouillon cultures of the *Bacillus pestis*, very much the same as the agglutinative action of typhoid or cholera serum.

Serotherapeutics.—Yersin claims to have developed a serum in the horse which is not only **protective**, but also **curative**, when injected into the human being. His experiments, carried on in a number of cases, seem to indicate this serum to have some decided beneficial effect when administered early in the disease, the proportion of deaths in cases so treated being scarcely 8 per cent., whereas the mortality in non-inoculated cases is as high as 80 per cent. To obtain the blood-serum from horses, he immunizes them with the dead bouillon cultures of the *Bacillus pestis*.

Haffkine has practised on an extensive scale protective inoculations against bubonic plague by injections of dead cultures. This immunity seems to last for several weeks.

Recently, observations have demonstrated that Yersin serum has absolutely no protective or curative properties. Haffkine's protective inoculations are still held in favor, however.

QUESTIONS.

By whom and when was the *Bacillus pestis* discovered?
Describe this bacillus. Its mode of staining. Its principal biologic characters.
What temperature suits its growth best? What is the effect of high temperature?
How does it grow on gelatin? On agar? On bouillon?
What is its behavior with regard to fermentation and to indol production?
How does it affect milk?
How is it affected by disinfectants?
What animals are susceptible to this disease?
How are inoculations performed?
Describe the symptoms and lesions caused by inoculation.
What three forms of bubonic plague are recognized in man? Which is the most frequent? Which the most fatal?
How does infection take place?
What are the symptoms of the disease, and what the lesions in man?
How is immunity conferred in this disease?
Does the serum in cases of plague contain agglutinating power?
How does Yersin manufacture his protective serum? What does he claim for it?
How does Haffkine practise his protective inoculations?

CHAPTER XXI.

RELAPSING FEVER.

Spirillum Obermeieri.

History.—As early as 1873 **Obermeier discovered** in the blood of patients suffering from relapsing fever a long, spirillum-like microörganism, measuring from 20 to 30 mikrons, having the power of active motion. His observations have since been confirmed by a number of other investigators.

This spirillum, which has not been cultivated artificially, is **found** in the blood and spleen, but never in the secretions of patients affected with relapsing fever.

Morphology and Biology.—It **stains** readily by all the anilin dyes, but does not stain by Gram's method. It is actively motile and contains **no spores.**

In the blood it is found in **two forms**: (1) **during the pyrexia** as long twisted filaments; (2) **after the crisis** of the fever is reached it is seen in the leucocytes as short degenerated curved rods.

Pathogenesis.—This spirillum is not pathogenic to the lower animals, with the exception of the monkey.

Blood taken from patients during the paroxysm when inoculated in other individuals may give rise to relapsing fever.

One attack of the disease does not seem to confer immunity from future attacks, but rather renders the subject more susceptible.

QUESTIONS.

What microörganism is the cause of relapsing fever?
By whom and when was it discovered?
Describe it.
How does it stain?
May it be cultivated artificially?
Where is it found in cases of relapsing fever?
Is it motile?
Does it contain spores?
In what two forms is it found in the blood?
For what animals is it pathogenic?
May blood of relapsing fever give rise to other cases of the disease by inoculation?
Does one attack of relapsing fever confer immunity upon the subject?

CHAPTER XXII.

DYSENTERY, HOG CHOLERA, AND CHICKEN CHOLERA.

DYSENTERY.

Bacillus Dysentericæ.

History.—This bacillus **was first found** in the intestinal contents and in the visceral walls and mesenteric glands in cases of acute epidemics of dysentery by **Shiga**, in Japan in 1898, and this observation was **confirmed** afterward by **Flexner** in a study of dysentery of the Philippine Islands. It seems to belong to the typho-colon group.

Morphology.—The *Bacillus dysentericæ* is of medium size, with round ends, containing **no spores,** and having flagella. It **stains** by the ordinary anilin dyes, but not by Gram's method.

Biologic Characters.—It is **aërobic,** but may be grown without oxygen. It grows at the ordinary room temperature, but best at the temperature of the human body, and does not liquefy gelatin.

Its growth on **agar** is not characteristic, slightly resembling the typhoid growth, and on **gelatin** the growth is pearl colored somewhat like the typhoid, but later becomes moist. On **potato** it sometimes has also an invisible growth; at other times its growth is rather voluminous and grayish brown in color. It clouds **bouillon** without forming a pellicle on the surface. It causes **no fermentation,** though it causes a slight increase of acidity in glucose-bouillon. It does not liquefy **blood-serum. Litmus milk** at the end of three days becomes of a pale lilac color, but the milk is not coagulated. In six or seven days the medium becomes dark blue. It produces **no indol.**

Agglutination.—The serum of affected animals has an agglutinating power on young cultures of the bacillus.

It is **pathogenic** for laboratory animals. When **injected intraperitoneally** into animals it produces a purulent peritonitis, with involvement of the mesenteric glands and swollen spleen, and the liver is covered with an exudate. The intestinal glands and Peyer's patches show signs of inflammation. The bacillus may be recovered from the exudate, and also in limited quantity from the organs. **Subcutaneous injections** show swelling and œdema at the point of inoculation, with involvement of the lymphatic glands, and are also followed by effusion in the serous cavities.

By alkalinizing the secretions of the stomach, animals have been infected **by feeding** with the bacillus, and in those animals lesions very much resembling the disease in man have been reproduced, and pure cultures of the bacillus obtained from the secretions of the intestines.

That the **poison is in the cell-body** of the *Bacillus dysentericæ,* and is not a secretion of the cells, is demonstrated by the fact that by heating cultures to a temperature above 60° C., which kills the bacilli, does not seem to have any effect on the activity of the poison.

Protective inoculations in animals have been performed with positive results, and the serum of immunized animals has been found to possess the **power of agglutination**, and to be both protective and curative.

HOG CHOLERA.

Bacillus Sui Pestifer.

History.—In the dejecta of hogs affected with cholera **Salmon** and **Smith** have succeeded in isolating a bacillus which they found to be the specific cause of this disease.

Morphology.—It is a short, thick rod, 1.20 to 1.50 mikrons in length, and 0.6 to 0.7 mikron in breadth, actively motile, containing flagella, **stains** by all the anilin dyes, but not by Gram's method.

Biologic Characters.—It is **aërobic** and grows in all the culture-media. Its growth on **gelatin** is visible in from twenty-four to forty-eight hours; the colonies appear irregularly round and the gelatin is not liquefied. On **agar-agar** the colonies are translucent and rather circumscribed. Upon **potato** the colonies are yellow. **Bouillon** is clouded and a thin surface growth may be observed. In **milk** it does not generate acids and does not coagulate it.

It **produces gas** copiously, but **no indol.**

Vitality.—It withstands drying for a long time. Its thermal death-point is 54° C.

Pathogenesis.—It is intensely pathogenic for every laboratory animal, death being preceded always by a rise of temperature, and **postmortem lesions** affecting chiefly the liver and kidneys are seen. Sometimes the lesions are found in the intestines and Peyer's glands also. The bacillus is found in all the organs. Artificially swine are inoculated with difficulty.

Immunity in animals has been produced by Salmon and Smith by injections of gradually increasing doses of cultures of this bacillus. De Schweinitz has isolated from cultures of the bacteria pure toxic substances with which he has been able to produce immunity. By subcutaneous inoculations with these toxins in cows he was able to develop in their blood-serum an antitoxic substance capable of protecting animals from the disease. The serum of infected animals has a remarkable **agglutinating power**; with a dilution of 1 to 10,000, agglutination can be obtained in an hour.

CHICKEN CHOLERA.

Bacillus Choleræ Gallinarum.

History.—This bacillus was observed by **Perroncito,** in 1878, and **described** by Pasteur.

The **cause** of the disease known in fowls as chicken cholera is due to a short, broad bacillus, with rounded ends, occurring singly or united to form filaments.

This bacillus **stains** in a peculiar way with the anilin dyes, its two poles being markedly stained, whereas the centre of the bacillus is scarcely stained at all, giving it very much the appearance of a micrococcus, which it was at first believed to be by Pasteur. It does not stain by Gram's method.

Biology.—It produces **no spores** and is non-motile. It is easily killed by heat and drying. It grows on all ordinary culture-media. On **gelatin** in two days the cultures appear to the naked eye as small white points; under the microscope the colonies are granular and concentric. It does not liquefy gelatin. In stab-cultures its growth on this media resembles that of a nail with a flat head, the head of the nail being closer to the surface of the medium than the point.

Its growth in **agar** and **bouillon** offers nothing characteristic. The bacillus is strictly **aërobic.**

Pathogenesis.—Chickens, geese, pigeons, sparrows, mice, and rabbits are susceptible animals. Guinea-pigs are immune. **By inoculation** the disease produced in susceptible animals is that of a general septicæmia, the bacillus being found in the blood and all the internal organs.

By feeding the contaminated material to animals the lesions are limited to the intestines, having the appearance of true cholera.

Protective inoculations have been performed by using attenuated cultures, the attenuation being arrived at, as recommended by Pasteur, by using cultures two or three months old. This bacillus has been used extensively in Australia for the destruction of rabbits. It is said that with two gallons of a bouillon culture as many as 2000 rabbits may be destroyed.

This bacillus has been described by different authors under a number of names: as the **bacillus of rabbit septicæmia,** by Koch; the **bacillus of swine plague,** by Loeffler; **Bacilli cunicucilidi,** by Fluegge, and others.

QUESTIONS.

Dysentery.

When and by whom was the *Bacillus dysentericæ* discovered and described?
What is its morphology?
How does it stain?
Give its principal biologic characters.
How does it grow on agar? On potato? On bouillon? In litmus milk?
Does it produce indol?
Does its serum have an agglutinating power?
What is the effect of an intraperitoneal injection in animals? Of a subcutaneous injection?
How are animals affected by feeding of the bacilli?
Where is the toxin of the *Bacilius dysentericæ* contained?
May animals be immunized against dysentery by inoculation with *Bacillus dysentericæ?*
What claims are made for the serum of inoculated animals?

Hog Cholera.

By whom was the bacillus of hog cholera discovered?
Give its morphology. Its staining. Its principal biologic characters.
How does it grow on gelatin and agar? On potato? In bouillon? In milk?
Does it produce gases?
What is its thermal death-point?
How does it affect laboratory animals?
Has immunity been produced by injections of cultures of this bacillus?
Has a toxin been isolated from the bacillus of hog cholera?
What are the properties of the serum of immunized animals?

Chicken Cholera.

By whom was the *Bacillus choleræ gallinarum* discovered, and by whom described?

Describe this bacillus.

How does it stain?

Give its principal biologic characters.

What is the appearance of the cultures on gelatin to the naked eye? How do they look when seen under the microscope?

What animals are subject to infection? Which animals are immune?

What sort of infection is produced in animals by the inoculation of this bacillus?

What is effected by feeding animals with material contaminated with this bacillus?

How are protective inoculations performed?

To what extent is this bacillus pathogenic to rabbits?

Under what different names has this bacillus been described by various authors?

CHAPTER XXIII.

THE PATHOGENIC MICROÖRGANISMS OTHER THAN BACTERIA.

ACTINOMYCOSIS, MALARIA, AND AMŒBIC COLITIS.

Streptothrix.

THE **streptothrix group,** which has not as yet been clearly defined, presents a number of varieties which have been found pathogenic. This group of microörganisms resembles the bacteria, yet differ from them in a number of important respects, and are associated, on the other hand, with the moulds. **They resemble the moulds** in so far that they develop from spore-like bodies into dichotomously branching threads, which grow into colonies having more or less the appearance of true mycelia. Under favorable conditions some of the threads become fruit hyphæ and break up into a number of spore-like bodies. These sporiform bodies differ from bacterial spores in the fact that they are stained by the ordinary method of staining. **They resemble the bacteria** in the fact that they occur as threads which may under careful cultivation become divided into short segments. They do not have a double wall like the moulds, and are not filled with fluid containing granules, and the segments of the filaments have no distinct partition separating one from the other.

The **most thoroughly studied streptothrices** are: the *Streptothrix actinomyces*, or ray fungus, the *Streptothrix maduræ*, and the *Streptothrix Eppingeri*, all of which have been found associated with important pathological lesions and are believed to be the cause of special diseases. *The bacteria of tuberculosis and diphtheria are believed by some to belong to the class of streptothrices, because at times they show a tendency to form branched segments. This view, however, is not generally accepted. It is interesting to note that the lesions caused by the streptothrix have very much the appearance of tuberculous lesions, being almost indistinguishable from tuberculosis except for the absence of the Bacillus tuberculosis.*

In diseases attributable to these fungi, **microscopical examinations of the tissues** reveal the streptothrices in the tissues, and these have been cultivated artificially, and by inoculations into animals have reproduced lesions identical with those of the original disease.

The most important of the diseases caused by one of the streptothrices, and the only one which will be studied in this volume, is:

ACTINOMYCOSIS.

Streptothrix Actinomyces (Ray Fungus).

History.—It was described first by **Bollinger,** in 1877, and found in the disease of cattle known as big-jaw or wooden-tongue, and contained in the tissues and exudates. **In man** the disease first **described** by **Israel,** in 1885, seems to be identical with this cattle disease.

Morphology.—In pus from the affected parts are small yellowish granular masses from 2 to 5 millimeters in diameter. Under the microscope these granules are seen to consist of a number of threads which radiate from a centre to a bulbous, club-like termination, the whole mass having very much the appearance of a rosette. Sometimes the free ends of the thread are only slightly or not at all swollen (Fig. 69). The threads which compose the centre of the mass are from 0.3 to 0.5 mikron in width. The clubs are from 0.6 to 0.8 mikron in width. These mycelia **stain** by all the ordinary anilin colors, and also by Gram's method, though by these methods their fine structure is not always brought out. The best stain for the fungus is **Mallory's stain**, which is as follows:

Stain the secretions on the slide with gentian-violet, dehydrate, and clear with anilin oil to which a little basic fuchsin

FIG. 69.

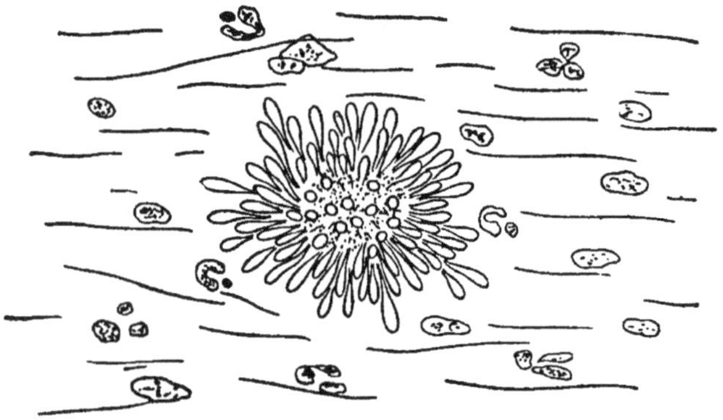

Actinomycosis fungus in pus. Fresh, unstained preparation. Magnified about 500 diameters. (Abbott.)

has been added, and mount in xylol balsam. In this way the cocci in the centre and the threads of the mycelium are stained blue; the club-like extremities are stained red.

Biologic Characters.—The *Streptothrix actinomyces* grows in all the ordinary artificial media, but from the fact that all the mycelia seen under the microscope are not living, it is often necessary to make several cultures before obtaining a satisfactory one. It grows both with and without oxygen, either at the room temperature or at the temperature of the incubator, and is not resistant to heat, being **destroyed** by a temperature of 75° C. in five minutes.

Its growth on **blood-serum** and **agar** is as isolated colonies on the surface of these media. The colonies are yellowish red and covered with a sort of fluffy down. After a few weeks the colonies run together and form a thick wrinkled mass which sinks into the media.

On **gelatin** the growth causes slow liquefaction. On **potato** the colony is yellowish red and limited in extent, has a viscid, membranous appearance, and is slow in progress. In **bouillon** it causes no clouding, but develops on the surface of the medium as a distinct granular growth forming a membranous film, which afterward sinks to the bottom of the tube.

Pathogenesis.—Cattle are the most frequently affected animals, though the disease has been seen in swine, dogs, and horses. The common location of the disease is in the jaw. It is not transmissible from animal to man. Inoculations of pure cultures are negative, though some observers have succeeded by intravascular inoculations in producing tumors from which the fungus was obtained in pure cultures.

The disease is sometimes quite prevalent among animals, and appears to result from the ingestion of vegetable products which contain the streptothrix.

In the earliest stages the parasites give rise to small tumors resembling tuberculous growths, and as these reach a larger size there is proliferation of the surrounding connective tissue. The tumors are then very hard, resembling osteosarcomata. Suppuration finally takes place, due to the action of the fungus itself, or more probably to secondary infection of the tumor by pus-producing organisms.

The Other Pathogenic Streptothrices.

The **streptothrix** of **madura foot**, described by Wright, in the *Journal of Experimental Medicine*, 1898, and the **Streptothrix farcinicus**, discovered by Nocard in 1888, in a disease of cattle resembling farcy in horses; the **Streptothrix Eppingeri**, discovered by Eppinger in a case of acute abscess of the brain; and the **Streptothrix pseudotuberculosa**, described by Flexner in 1897, are of interest, and the reader is referred to larger works on Bacteriology for their description.

MALARIA.

Plasmodium Malariæ.

History.—In 1880 **Laveran discovered** in the blood of cases of intermittent fever a microörganism which he believed to be the cause of this disease. This microörganism belongs to the animal kingdom of the **family of the protozoa,** and has received a number of names. The one generally applied to-day is that of **Plasmodium malariæ.**

Later investigations have shown that this protozoa has **two cycles of existence.** One cycle is **reproduced in man,** and the other cycle in the body of some insects of the **mosquito tribe,** the **Anopheles claviger** or **Anopheles maculapennis.**

In the red blood-corpuscles of man the parasites go through an undetermined number of life-cycles, and then pass into the middle intestine of certain species of mosquitoes, in which they go through the various phases of a new life-cycle, ending in the salivary glands, and from these when the mosquito bites a human being, in order to obtain nourishment, the parasite passes again into man.

The phase of life which is completed in man is the cause of malarial fever. In the younger stages the parasites in this life-cycle appear as very small amœboid bodies, which have a more or less rapid motion, and which are found in the red blood-corpuscles, nourishing themselves with the substance of these corpuscles and converting their hæmoglobin into a black pigment known as **melanin.** They increase in size, cease their motion, and by a process of fission multiply; the daughter cells resulting from this fission become free in the plasma and invade other blood-corpuscles, in which they go through the same life-cycle.

The **two principal symptoms of malaria,** anæmia and intermittent fever, are related to this life-cycle, the anæmia being due to the destruction of a large number of the red blood-corpuscles by the parasites, and the fever is manifested when the parasite is undergoing multiplication.

In their growth the parasites of malaria have been shown

to belong to **different varieties**, differing in their appearance, their mode of division, and the length of time which they take to go through their whole life-cycle. Three varieties are at present recognized: the **tertian**, which goes through its life-cycle in man in forty-eight hours; the **quartan**, whose life-cycle is three days; and the **æstivo-autumnal**, whose life-cycle is indefinite and irregular.

These different species have **constant characteristics**, and are not transformed from one into another, though Laveran claims that they are modifications of one and the same species, and are interchangeable. Recent researches have demonstrated that each variety of malarial parasite is the cause of a particular kind of malarial fever, and by a microscopic examination of the blood of a patient one may authoritatively state the kind of malaria with which that patient is affected.

In addition to the life-cycle which begins and ends in the human subject, there is another one which only begins in man. For instance, some of the parasite bodies increase in size; they do not divide, but getting free in the blood-plasma they are found as bodies of characteristic shape, larger than the red blood-corpuscles. These bodies circulate in the blood for a number of days, not giving rise to any phenomena; and if they remain sterile, they degenerate and disappear. Upon examination it is found that some of those bodies throw off flagella which move with great rapidity among the red blood-corpuscles; others do not present this phenomenon. In the æstivo-autumnal parasites, on account of their appearance these bodies have been called **crescent bodies**. Some persons regard these forms as degenerated forms; but it has been definitely ascertained that those bodies which degenerate and disappear, when they remain in man are capable in the intestines of certain species of mosquitoes of starting a second life-cycle which may be described as follows: When a mosquito of the *Anopheles* variety bites a person in whose blood these crescent bodies are present, or their analogous form in the other species of parasites, some of them are taken up with the blood and lodge in the mid-intestine of the mosquito. Certain of these crescent-forms give out flagella which are motile filaments containing chromatin, and these loose filaments penetrate and fecundate other crescent-forms. And the fecundated bodies are after this able to penetrate the epithelium of the intestines and travel between the muscular fibres of the intestines. *There is therefore a differentiation of sex between the crescent bodies:* those becoming flagellated are the male elements, the **microgametocytes**; and the others, which do not become flagellated, are **macrogametes**, the female. These macrogametes after fecundation develop between the muscles of the intestines of the mosquito, becoming surrounded with a capsule and acquiring the characteristics of **typical sporozoa.** After a while its nucleus divides into a number of smaller ones, which in their turn become the nucleus of the dividing cell itself, the **sporozoite.** These sporozoites are set free by rupture of the capsule of the sporozoa, and are scattered throughout the body of the mosquito, some finding lodgement in the tubules of the salivary glands, and when the insect again stings man, sporozoites are inoculated into him together with the irritating secretion of the gland.

This **cycle lasts** in the mosquito from eight to ten days, and varies with the species of the parasite. It is likely that this represents the whole life of the malarial parasite, and it has been demonstrated that the infected mosquito does not transmit the malarial parasite to its larva, the two life-cycles in man and the mosquito being sufficient to explain the known practical facts.

The **three varieties of the malarial parasites found in the human blood** differ as to size, distribution of their pigments, in the number of daughter cells produced from one parasite, and the length of time required for the completion of their life-cycle. One form, the **tertian,** requires forty-eight hours; another, the **quartan,** requires seventy-two hours; and a third form, the **æstivo-autumnal,** has an indefinite life-cycle. Occasionally there are seen what are known as the **double-tertian** and **double-quartan** forms of malarial fever, in which the fever is produced by several generations of one of those two forms of parasites going through their life-cycles beginning at different times and on successive days, so that the fever has the appearance of a **quotidian** form of fever. The three different varieties of parasites will be best understood by referring to the figures on Plate VI.

Examination of the Blood of Man for Diagnostic Purposes.—The following two methods always serve best: (1) the fresh blood examination and (2) the examination of stained specimens. Whenever practicable, **fresh blood examination** offers the easiest and best method for diagnosis.

The **technic** is as follows: Thoroughly clean cover-glasses and slides, being careful to remove all greasy matter. Cleanse also the skin of the lobe of the ear or tip of a finger, make an incision with a sharp-pointed knife, wipe off the first exuding drop, touch the top of the next drop with a clean cover-glass held with forceps, being careful to avoid touching the skin, and taking the drop when small so that the corpuscles will be spread out in a uniform layer, not in rouleaux, when the cover-glass is laid on the slide; press the cover-glass on to the slide gently; if the cover-glass and slide are clean, the blood will spread in an even thin layer; examine with a $\frac{1}{12}$ oil-immersion. Preparations made in this way will show, if examined immediately, the amœboid plasmodium inside of the red blood-cells, being especially recognizable by the movements or the contained pigment. It is possible sometimes to keep such preparations for several hours.

When examination of fresh blood is not practicable, or when it is desired to preserve the preparation, resort to the **procedure of staining** must be had. This is best accomplished by the methylene-blue and eosin methods, either applied together, or each dye being used separately, as follows:

A drop of blood is taken as just described, spread evenly upon a thin cover-glass, and allowed to air-dry; the film is then set by immersing the cover-glass for twenty to thirty minutes in a mixture of equal parts of absolute alcohol and ether; after drying, the mixed stain (methylene-blue and eosin) is applied over the surface of the film and allowed to remain for five minutes; it is then poured off, the preparation washed

PLATE VI.

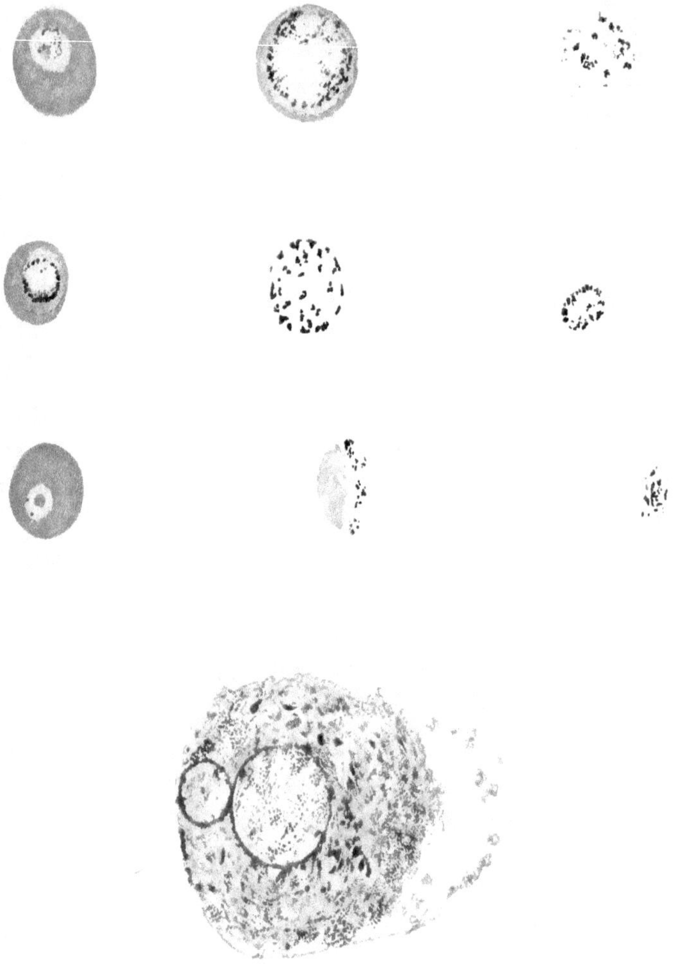

FIGS. 1, 2, and 3 show three phases of the parasite of tertian fever. Fig. 1, ring form, showing beginning pigment formation. Fig. 2, full-grown parasite. Fig. 3, segmenting bodies. (WELCH and THAYER.)

FIGS. 4, 5, and 6 show the parasite of quartan fever at different stages of growth. Fig. 4, moderately developed intracorpuscular parasite. Fig. 5, large swollen extracorpuscular form. Fig. 6, flagellate body. (WELCH and THAYER.)

FIGS. 7, 8, and 9 illustrate the æstivo-autumnal parasite. Fig. 7, ring-like body, with a few pigmented granules. Fig. 8, crescent still in blood-corpuscle. Fig. 9, vacuolation of crescent. (WELCH and THAYER.)

FIG. 10. Amœba from section of intestine hardened in alcohol and stained with methylene blue. (COUNCILMAN and LAFLEUR.)

thoroughly in distilled water three or four times, then dried and mounted in balsam, and examined. *In this preparation the red cells will be stained pink, the leucocytes pale blue and their nuclei dark blue; the parasites will be stained very dark blue and their pigment-granules remain unstained.*

The mixture of methylene-blue and eosin is prepared as follows:

Saturated aqueous solution of methyl-blue, 1 part;
Alcoholic solution of eosin (1 per cent.), 2 parts.
Do not filter.

Loeffler's methylene-blue, and Ehrlich's hæmatoxylin and eosin, give also at times very excellent preparations.

The varieties of plasmodia may be distinguished from each other.

Differentiation between the Tertian and Quartan Parasites:

1st. The tertian parasite completes its life-cycle in two days; that of the quartan requires three days.

2d. The tertian parasite has a tendency to discolor the blood-cells and to enlarge them. The quartan does not discolor so much, and never enlarges its containing red cell; on the contrary, the cell generally appears smaller.

3d. The quartan parasite has better-defined and clearer outlines and coarser pigment-granules than the tertian.

4th. In fission the quartan parasite divides into six to twelve daughter cells, which are larger and contain each a refractive granule in its centre. The tertian parasite divides into fifteen to twenty daughter cells, smaller, and with no central granule.

Inoculation.—Blood infected with either kind of parasite when inoculated into healthy individuals has in a number of cases produced that variety of fever specific for the particular parasite, and this special parasite has been found in the blood of the inoculated individual.

AMŒBIC COLITIS.

Amœba Coli.

History.—In certain forms of chronic dysentery accompanied with ulcerations of the lower bowel, and which very often give rise to suppuration in internal organs, especially the liver, an animal parasite, the **Amœba coli**, has been accurately described since 1875 by **Losch**, of St. Petersburg. Losch's observations have been confirmed since by a number of other observers.

Morphology.—The amœba is a protozoa, and consists of protoplasm which exhibits under different conditions various forms. In the quiescent condition it is spherical in shape, and may be recognized from the other cellular elements by its greater refraction of light and by its pale-green color. Its size is from 10 to 25 mikrons. The body consists of two parts: an inner part, or **endoplasm**, which is generally granular and of dark color; and an outer part, or **ectoplasm**, which is pale and white. These two parts may be best made out in the motile amœba. A nucleus more or less central is also easily made out.

The *Amœba coli* is **stained** easily by any of the nucleolar stains, especially by methylene-blue. In its body may often be seen foreign bodies, especially red blood-cells, but it rarely contains leucocytes or fat.

The **motion of the amœba** is caused by the mechanism of **pseudopodia**, which are blunt homogeneous processes, the protrusion of a portion of the ectoplasm. Motion is sometimes gradual and deliberate, at other times rapid, and is modified by variations in temperature.

Biology.—Nothing is known as to the functions of **nutrition, respiration,** and **reproduction** of the amœba. It is found occasionally in health in the secretions of the lower bowel, and in cases of dysentery may disappear partially or completely from the stools during convalescence. They are also frequently found in the pus of hepatic abscesses.

Examination of the feces, especially the slimy portion of dysenteric stools, and the pus in cases of suspected amœbic infection, should be made in fresh specimens, when the live amœbæ may be easily recognized. Dried preparations are made as for bacterial examination, and colored with aqueous solution of methylene-blue.

QUESTIONS.

Streptothrix.

What is a streptothrix? How does it resemble moulds? How does it differ from moulds? How does it resemble bacteria?

Which are the best known of the streptothrices?

Why are the *Bacillus tuberculosis* and *Bacillus diphtheriæ* believed to belong to the class of the streptothrices?

What is the appearance of the lesion caused by streptothrices?

Describe the *Streptothrix actinomyces*, or ray fungus. How is it best stained? Give Mallory's staining method.

Give the principal biologic characters of the *Streptothrix actinomyces.*

How does it grow on blood-serum and agar? On gelatin? On potato? In bouillon?

What animals are susceptible to streptothrix infection? Is the disease transmissible from animal to animal or from animal to man? How are animals infected?

Describe the lesions produced by streptothrix infection. What causes the suppuration?

What other pathogenic streptothrices have been described and studied?

Malaria.

What is the *Plasmodium malariæ?*

How many life-cycles has it? Where are those phases of life completed?

Describe the life-cycle of the plasmodium in man.

What are the two principal symptoms of malaria, and what relation have they to the development of the parasite?

What differentiates the varieties of the malarial parasites from each other?

What three varieties are at present recognized?

What forms of fever are caused by these different varieties?

What life-cycle only begins in the body of man?

Describe the flagellated and non-flagellated bodies?

What are the crescent bodies?

How do those crescent bodies or their homologues develop in the body of the mosquito?

What are the microgametocytes?

What are the macrogametes?

Describe the development of the fecundated macrogametes in the mosquito?

What are the sporozoites, and how do they infect man?

What is the duration of the life-cycle parasite in the mosquito?

Does the mosquito transmit the malarial parasite to its larva?

What is meant by the double-tertian and double-quartan forms of malarial fever?

To what is the quotodian form of fever due?

Give the technic for the examination of fresh malarial blood for diagnostic purposes.

How are stained specimens prepared for examination?

What is the differentiation between the quartan and tertian parasite in the blood?

Is the blood of malarial patients infectious?

Amœba Coli.

Where is the *Amœba coli* found? To what kingdom does it belong? Describe it.

What is the endoplasm?

What is the ectoplasm?

How is *Amœba coli* stained?

What may be seen in the body of the *Amœba coli?*

What causes the motion of the amœba?

How is examination for the *Amœba coli* practised?

CHAPTER XXIV.

BACTERIOLOGICAL EXAMINATIONS OF WATER, AIR, AND SOIL.

THE BACTERIOLOGICAL INVESTIGATION OF WATER.

BOTH **qualitative** and **quantitative bacteriological examinations** of water are often resorted to in order to test the adaptability of this substance for human and animal consumption. By the **quantitative test** the number of bacteria present in the water is ascertained without any reference to their pathogenic character, and when this number exceeds **500 bacteria per c.c.** the water is condemned. This is evidently not a very fair test, but it is not without value when it is considered that in a number of instances the virulence of some pathogenic microörganisms is increased when they are inoculated together with saprophytic germs; and again, that the introduction of non-pathogenic bacteria occasionally so diminishes the animal resistance that animals resistant to inoculations by some pathogenic bacteria are subsequently rendered susceptible.

This quantitative analysis is especially useful in cases in which the mean quantity of bacteria in a given body of water is already known, and as a matter of comparison to ascertain whether any new source of contamination has been introduced.

The **examination is made as follows**: A sample of the water is collected in clean sterilized bottles or tubes. If the water is from a pump, well, or from a cistern, it should be allowed to run for a few minutes before the sample is taken. If the water is from a spring, river, or any collection of water, the sample for examination should be taken a foot or two below the surface of the water. Agar and gelatin plates should be immediately inoculated with the water. When this is not practicable the plates should be made at as early a time as possible, the samples meanwhile being kept on ice, near the freezing-point, to prevent the further development of bacteria.

For the purpose of collecting water for examination, glass bulbs after the pattern of Sternberg (Fig. 70) are very useful. These consist of a sphere blown on the end of a glass

FIG. 70.

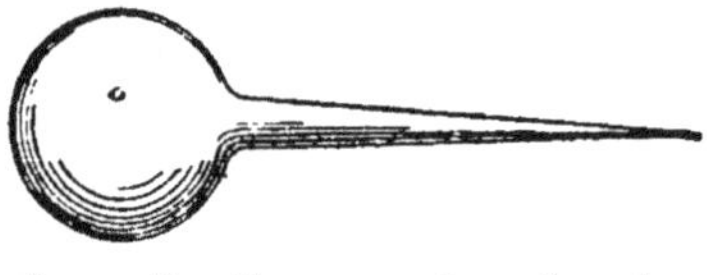

Glass bulb for collecting samples of water. (Abbott.)

tube, the stem at the other end terminating in a capillary tube. After thoroughly cleaning these bulbs, a negative vacuum is established therein by introducing in each tube a few drops of water, allowing same to boil over a gas-flame, and when the water has completely vaporized into steam the capillary end of the bulb is brought into the flame and the apparatus sealed. When it is desired to collect a sample of water, the capillary end of the bulb is broken under the water and the vacuum in the tube causes a suction of the fluid into the bulb until same is about three-fourths full. When this is accomplished, the bulb should again be sealed and packed in ice.

When making gelatin and agar plates a known quantity of water should always be used to each plate, say 0.01, 0.05, 0.10, or 1 c.c., the quantity varying according to the amount of suspected contamination of the water. The plates are made as already described in the chapter on the making of plates, only plate No. 1, however, being made. After twenty-four or forty-eight hours the colonies on the plate are counted; and as it is assumed that each colony is grown from a single bacterium, the number of colonies on the plate represents the number of bacteria originally in the sample. **Two sets of plates should always be made**, one on gelatin, which is kept at the room temperature, and another on agar for the incubator. When the number of colonies on the plates is very large, plates should be made with still greater dilution, so as to obtain plates with only a moderate number of bacteria, in order to facilitate the count. Absolutely sterile water should always be used to make the dilution. In expressing results, the number of bacteria in 1 c.c. of the water is mentioned. For counting the colonies on the plates the **counter of Wolfhuegel** (Fig. 31) is used, which **consists of** a wooden framework, at the bottom of which may be put a glass plate, white or black, in order to form a background for the plate containing the colonies. Over this background the plate of which the colonies are to be counted is placed, and over this a transparent glass plate ruled in square centimeters, and held in position just above the colonies, but without touching them. It is easy in this way to count the colonies in each square centimeter, and so make out the total number of colonies on the plate. When this is found too tedious, a number of squares at different portions of the plate may be counted, an average established, and that average multiplied by the number of squares will give approximately the number of colonies on the plate. By multiplying the number of colonies on the plate according to the degree of dilution of the water, it is easy to arrive at the number of bacteria in a cubic centimeter of the water. Thus if the average number of colonies per square is 15, and there are 100 squares on the plate, and the amount of water used in making the plate was 0.10 c.c., then 15 × 100 × 10 equals 15,000, which represents the number of bacteria present in 1 c.c. of the water.

Petri dishes may be used instead of plates, and for the counting of colonies on the same special means have been

FIG. 71.

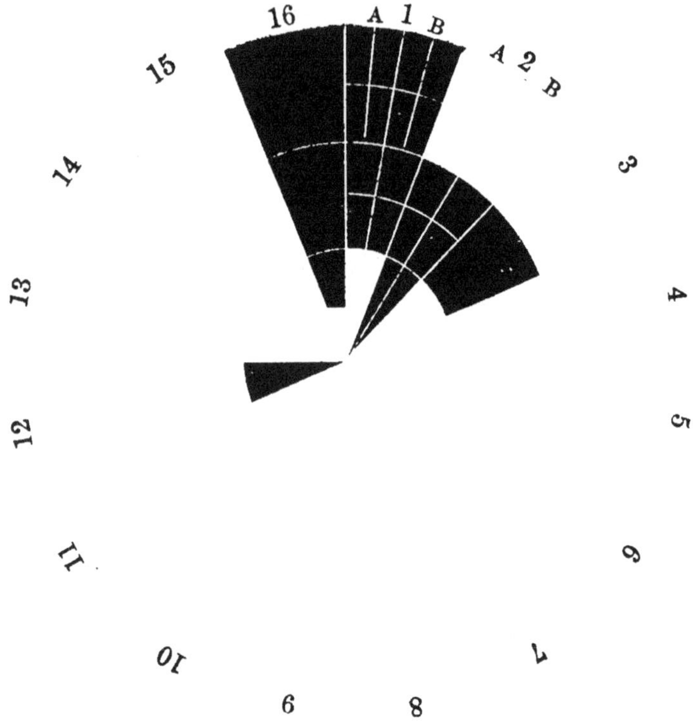

Pakes' apparatus for counting colonies (reduced one-third).

devised. That of **Pakes' apparatus** (Fig. 71) is a cheap and convenient one. It consists of a sheet of paper on which is printed a black disc ruled with white lines. The Petri dish is placed centrally upon this paper, and the colonies between the white lines are counted, the whole circle being divided into sixteen equal segments, as seen in the figure.

For **counting colonies,** a small **hand lens,** such as is represented in Fig. 72, is often necessary.

FIG. 72.

Lens for counting colonies.

Instead of plates and Petri dishes, **Esmarch tubes** may be used as follows: A definite quantity of the water is added to melted gelatin in a test-tube and the same rolled as described previously.

A **special counter for Esmarch tubes,** provided with a magnifying glass, is used in counting the colonies (Fig. 73).

FIG. 73.

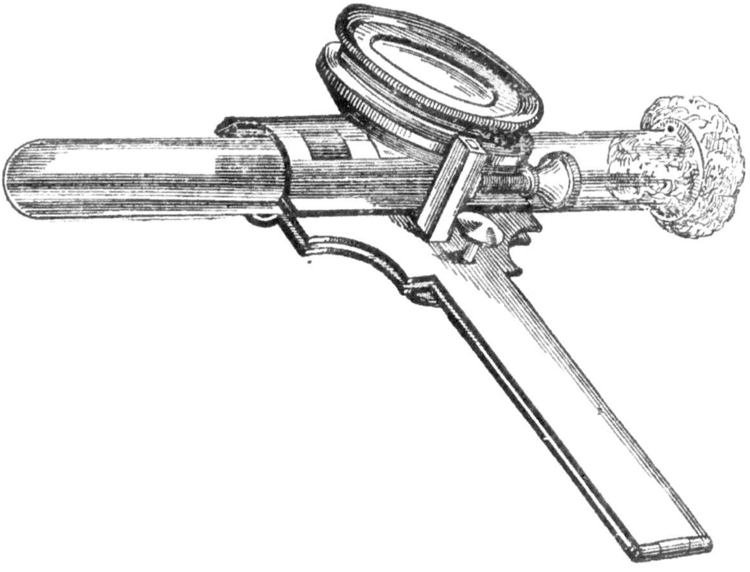

Esmarch's apparatus for counting colonies in rolled tubes. (Abbott.)

As previously mentioned, the value of **this quantitative examination of the bacteria of water** is not very great, because, though of great utility, it does not give definite information as to the poisonous organisms of the water. For this purpose a **qualitative examination for pathogenic germs** is of much more value. This is not, however, as easily performed, and in the great majority of cases gives negative results.

The **bacteria most often sought in** this way are the bacillus of cholera and the bacillus of typhoid fever, both of which are short-lived in water, and have only rarely been demonstrated, partly perhaps on account of their low vitality in water, and partly also because they are looked for at a date considerably later than that at which they were originally contained in the water. From the very nature of these bacteria it is easy to understand why they should be short-lived. The presence in the water of a number of **ordinary saprophytes** interferes with the growth of pathogenic bacteria, and either destroys them or consumes the pabulum necessary for their growth. **Sedimentation of the water,** which is constantly taking place, carries along with insoluble inorganic matter the bacteria to the bottom; and in running water the oxygen of the air and direct sunlight act as efficient germicides.

In **making qualitative examinations of water** for typhoid and cholera germs, what has been said in the special chapters on those germs should be borne in mind. It is advantageous, for instance, to mix the water with three times its volume of sterile bouillon, and to incubate this mixture before making the plates.

For **cholera,** after six hours in the incubator the plates may be made, taking for this purpose the fluid from the upper portion of the mixture, as this germ grows rapidly, and chiefly on the surface of the fluid.

For **typhoid fever** the incubation should be continued for two or three days before making the plates. By this incubation the ordinary saprophytes are retarded in growth, as they have less tendency to thrive at the incubator temperature, whereas the reverse is the case for pathogenic germs, which grow much more rapidly at 37° C., and are thus in relatively larger numbers. **Two sets of plates should be made** as described in the quantitative test, one to be kept at the room temperature and the other to be incubated, and after these have grown for twenty-four to forty-eight hours the colonies should be examined under a low power of the microscope, and the colonies picked up with a platinum needle and planted in fresh agar and gelatin tubes, and these plated again until pure cultures are obtained.

Elsner's method, described in the chapter on typhoid fever, is a very good method for the separation of water bacteria from typhoid bacteria, and the reader is referred to that chapter for its description.

The **addition of antiseptics,** in small amounts, helps in the recognition of pathogenic germs, such as typhoid, in water, as these antiseptics interfere more materially with the growth of saprophytes than they do with that of the pathogenic germs.

The reader is again reminded that the isolation of typhoid fever germs from water is difficult.

It is easier to examine water for the **Bacillus coli communis,** which when present shows contamination by animal or human excreta, and makes the water unfit for consumption.

By **inoculating glucose-** or **lactose-bouillon** in fermentation-tubes, the presence of this bacillus is easily made out on account of the rapid development of gases it produces; and plates made from the bouillon in the closed arm of the fermentation-tube will yield in such cases almost pure cultures of this bacillus.

BACTERIOLOGICAL EXAMINATION OF THE AIR.

A number of methods have been suggested for this purpose; some consist in exposing plates of nutrient media, such as gelatin and agar, in the air, the bacteria falling on these plates and developing; or, again, causing by slow aspiration a measured volume of air to pass through substances, such as sterilized sand or granulated sugar, afterward making agar and gelatin plate cultures with them. Quiet air contains but few bacteria, but air in motion, as in blowing wind, carries solid substances, such as dirt, etc., loaded with bacteria. These may travel in suspension in the air for a considerable distance.

The **Sedgwick-Tucker method** is perhaps the best procedure for the examination of air.

For this purpose an apparatus known as the **aërobioscope** (Fig. 74) is required. In this apparatus a certain amount of sterile dry granulated sugar is introduced into the narrow part of the tube at *d;* and at *a* a small roll of fine brass wire-gauze is inserted in order to provide a stop for the filtering material which is placed over it, as, for example, the sugar; then by means of an air-pump a certain definite quantity of air is sucked through the aërobioscope, after which the apparatus is closed with sterile cotton at

FIG. 74.

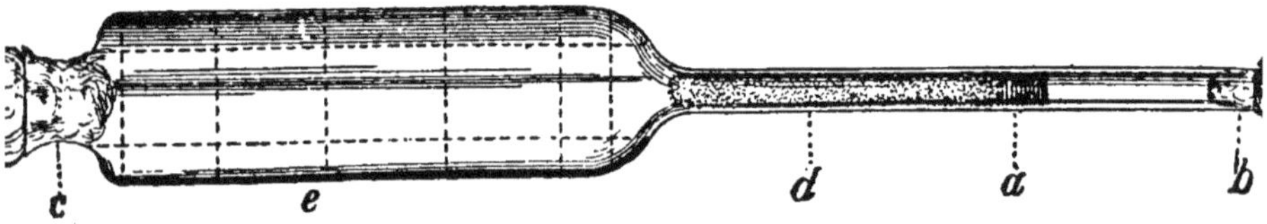

The Sedgwick-Tucker aërobioscope. (Abbott.)

b and at *c*, and by gentle tapping, the contaminated sugar is forced into the larger portion of the tube at *e;* when this is accomplished 20 c.c. of liquefied sterile gelatin are poured in the larger part of the tube, the sugar dissolved in this gelatin, and an ordinary Esmarch tube made. The colonies may be counted as in an Esmarch tube, and pure cultures of the isolated colonies may be made on other plates.

THE BACTERIOLOGICAL EXAMINATION OF THE SOIL.

In the study of the soil for microörganisms special instruments for collecting the soil at different depths have been invented. **C. Fraenkel's apparatus** is perhaps the most useful.

Small fragments of the soil to be examined should be dissolved in liquid gelatin or agar, plates made, and the colonies counted as for the examination of water.

The **objection to this method**, however, lies in the fact that the solid particles of earth interfere considerably with the counting of the colonies, and to obviate this it is necessary at times to dissolve the soil in a certain quantity of sterile water, and to make plate cultures from this water.

It should always be remembered, however, in making examinations of the soil, that a number of the bacteria found in it are anaërobics, and should be cultivated as such.

Soil taken near the surface is always rich in bacteria, and the further down the investigator proceeds the smaller is the number of bacteria found, until at a distance of a meter and a half from the surface all bacteria have disappeared.

In examinations of excavations made in the city of New Orleans some three years ago the author had occasion to verify the foregoing fact fully; cultures made from mud at different depths showed a constant diminution of micro-organisms, until at a depth of between five and six feet no bacteria could be obtained.

QUESTIONS.

What sort of bacteriological examinations of water are made?
What is meant by a quantitative test?
Why is this not a fair test?
How is a quantitative analysis of water made?
What instrument is useful for that purpose?
How should water be collected?
What dilutions should be used?
How is this dilution made?
How are the colonies on plates counted?
Describe Wolfhuegel's apparatus for counting colonies on plates?
How are Petri dishes used?
Describe Pakes' apparatus for counting colonies in Petri dishes.
How are Esmarch tubes made?
For what bacteria is the qualitative analysis of water made?
What are the difficulties in making qualitative analysis?
How is examination of water for the cholera germ made? For typhoid fever germ?
Describe Elsner's method of examining water for typhoid fever bacilli.
What influence has the addition of antiseptics to water for bacterial examination?
How is water to be examined for the presence of *Bacillus coli communis?*
What is the significance of the *Bacillus coli communis* in water?
Describe a method for the bacteriological examination of air.
Describe Sedgwick-Tucker's method.
How is an examination of the soil made?
What bacteria are found in the soil?
At what depth from the surface is the soil free from bacteria?

INDEX.